# Designing to FIPS-140

## A Guide for Engineers
## and Programmers

David Johnston
Richard Fant

Apress®

*Designing to FIPS-140: A Guide for Engineers and Programmers*

David Johnston
Hillsboro, OR, USA

Richard Fant
Austin, TX, USA

ISBN-13 (pbk): 979-8-8688-0124-2
https://doi.org/10.1007/979-8-8688-0125-9

ISBN-13 (electronic): 979-8-8688-0125-9

Managing Director, Apress Media LLC: Welmoed Spahr
Acquisitions Editor: Susan McDermott
Development Editor: Laura Berendson
Project Manager: Jessica Vakili

Cover image designed by Freepik (www.freepik.com)

Distributed to the book trade worldwide by Springer Science+Business Media New York, 1 New York Plaza, Suite 4600, New York, NY 10004-1562, USA. Phone 1-800-SPRINGER, fax (201) 348-4505, e-mail orders-ny@springer-sbm.com, or visit www.springeronline.com. Apress Media, LLC is a California LLC and the sole member (owner) is Springer Science + Business Media Finance Inc (SSBM Finance Inc). SSBM Finance Inc is a **Delaware** corporation.

For information on translations, please e-mail booktranslations@springernature.com; for reprint, paperback, or audio rights, please e-mail bookpermissions@springernature.com.

Apress titles may be purchased in bulk for academic, corporate, or promotional use. eBook versions and licenses are also available for most titles. For more information, reference our Print and eBook Bulk Sales web page at http://www.apress.com/bulk-sales.

Any source code or other supplementary material referenced by the authors in this book is available to readers on GitHub. For more detailed information, please visit https://www.apress.com/gp/services/source-code.

Paper in this product is recyclable

# Table of Contents

About the Authors ............................................................................................. xi

Acknowledgments ........................................................................................... xiii

Introduction ......................................................................................................xv

Chapter 1: Introduction to FIPS and CMVP ................................................... 1

1.1 What Is FIPS 140-3? ................................................................................... 1

1.2 The Major Tasks in FIPS Design ................................................................. 3

    1.2.1 FIPS Module Definitions ...................................................................... 3

    1.2.2 Hardware Module .................................................................................. 5

    1.2.3 Software Module ................................................................................... 6

    1.2.4 Firmware Module .................................................................................. 8

    1.2.5 Software-Hardware Hybrid Module ....................................................... 9

    1.2.6 Firmware-Hardware Hybrid Module ................................................... 11

    1.2.7 Firmware vs. Software ........................................................................ 13

    1.2.8 Security-Level Definitions .................................................................. 13

1.3 FIPS Pitfalls to Avoid ............................................................................... 16

    1.3.1 Documentation .................................................................................... 17

1.4 Most Common Pitfalls ............................................................................... 17

1.5 Glossary/Abbreviations ............................................................................. 20

Chapter 2: Core Concepts ............................................................................. 23

2.1 FIPS 140 Module ...................................................................................... 23

2.2 FIPS/Cryptographic Boundary .................................................................. 23

2.3 SSPs .......................................................................................................... 25

2.4 Security Policy .......................................................................................... 26

2.5 Self-Tests .................................................................................................. 26

2.6 Zeroization ......................................................................................... 27

2.7 Life Cycle Assurance .......................................................................... 28

2.8 Finite State Model .............................................................................. 28

**Chapter 3: Finite State Models ................................................... 29**

3.1 Mandatory States ............................................................................... 33

    3.1.1 Power On/Off State ..................................................................... 33

    3.1.2 General Initialization State............................................................ 33

    3.1.3 Crypto Officer State ..................................................................... 34

    3.1.4 CSP Entry State ........................................................................... 35

    3.1.5 User State.................................................................................... 35

    3.1.6 Approved State ............................................................................ 35

    3.1.7 Self-Test State ............................................................................. 36

    3.1.8 Error State ................................................................................... 36

    3.1.9 Optional States ........................................................................... 38

3.2 Other States You Are Going to Need.................................................... 39

**Chapter 4: Approved Algorithms ................................................. 43**

4.1 Block Ciphers...................................................................................... 44

    4.1.1 AES ............................................................................................ 45

    4.1.2 Two-Key TDEA............................................................................. 46

    4.1.3 TDEA/3DES ................................................................................ 46

4.2 Block Cipher Modes of Operation........................................................ 47

    4.2.1 Block Cipher Privacy Modes ........................................................ 47

    4.2.2 Block Cipher Authentication Modes.............................................. 48

    4.2.3 Block Cipher Authenticated Encryption Modes (AEAD Modes) ...................................... 48

4.3 Hash Functions ................................................................................... 49

    4.3.1 The SHA-1 Hash Function............................................................ 51

    4.3.2 SHA224 and SHA256 Hash Functions.......................................... 51

    4.3.3 SHA384, SHA512, SHA512/224, SHA512/256 Hash Functions ..................................... 52

    4.3.4 SHA3 Hash Function ................................................................... 52

    4.3.5 SHAKE128 and SHAKE256............................................................ 53

4.3.6 SHA3 Derived Functions ...................................................................... 54

4.3.7 TupleHash .................................................................................................... 54

4.3.8 ParallelHash ................................................................................................ 55

4.4 Limitations of Hash Use in SP800-90A ....................................................... 56

4.4.1 Permitted Hashes in SP800-90A DRBGs ................................................ 56

4.4.2 Disallowed Hashes in SP800-90A DRBGs.............................................. 57

4.5 Message Authentication Codes..................................................................... 57

4.5.1 CBC-MAC Cipher Block Chaining Message Authentication Code........... 57

4.5.2 CMAC (Cipher-Based Message Authentication Code) ............................ 58

4.5.3 HMAC Keyed-Hash Message Authentication Code ................................. 60

4.5.4 KMAC ........................................................................................................... 60

4.6 Key Derivation Functions .............................................................................. 60

4.6.1 KDF in Counter Mode................................................................................. 61

4.6.2 KDF in Feedback Mode .............................................................................. 62

4.6.3 KDF in Double Pipeline Iteration Mode ................................................... 62

4.6.4 Password-Based Key Derivation .............................................................. 63

4.6.5 FIPS 198-1 Hash-Based Key Derivation Function.................................. 67

4.7 Deterministic Random Bit Generators.......................................................... 68

**Chapter 5: Counter Security Features of NIST-Approved Cryptographic Algorithms** .......................................................................................................... **69**

5.1 General Principles of Poor Cryptographic Design ....................................... 69

5.1.1 Overly Flexible Compliant Implementation Choices ............................... 69

5.1.2 Excessively Repetitive Use of Security-Critical Data.............................. 70

5.1.3 Focusing on Algorithm Transition over Data Encoding Transition ......... 70

5.1.4 Unjustified Use of Overcomplicated Cryptographic Algorithms.............. 71

5.1.5 KDF Double Pipeline Iteration Mode ........................................................ 71

5.1.6 SP800-90A Block Cipher DF ..................................................................... 72

5.1.7 SP800-90A HMAC and HASH DRBGs ...................................................... 72

5.1.8 CTR-DRBG.................................................................................................... 72

5.1.9 AES ............................................................................................................... 73

**Chapter 6: CAVP Lab** ....................................................................... **75**

6.1 CAVP Tool Overview ..................................................................... 75

    6.1.1 CAVS Tool ........................................................................... 76

    6.1.2 Automated Cryptographic Validation Test System ..................... 76

6.2 First-Party CAVP Lab .................................................................. 80

    6.2.1 First-Party Lab vs. Third-Party Lab ...................................... 81

    6.2.2 Setting Up a First-Party CAVP Lab ....................................... 84

**Chapter 7: ACVTS Testing** .............................................................. **87**

7.1 Vendor Information and Implementation Document ......................... 88

7.2 Demo Vectors ............................................................................. 89

    7.2.1 AES-ECB Test Vector Request JSON ..................................... 90

    7.2.2 Demo Vector Expected and Response JSON ........................... 97

    7.2.3 Reading ACVTS Request Files ............................................ 103

    7.2.4 Comparing ACVTS Expected and Response JSON Files ........... 106

7.3 Other JSON Schema for ACVP ..................................................... 107

7.4 Example of a Real ACVP Certificate .............................................. 107

**Chapter 8: Entropy Assessment** ....................................................... **109**

8.1 What Is Entropy? ........................................................................ 109

8.2 Measuring Entropy of Finite Binary Sequences .............................. 111

8.3 Entropy of Non-full Entropy and Non-IID Binary Sequences ............ 112

8.4 MCV Entropy Analysis .................................................................. 117

8.5 Actual Min-Entropy vs. Lower Bound Min-Entropy .......................... 119

8.6 IID vs. Non-IID ............................................................................ 119

    8.6.1 Permutation Testing ........................................................... 120

8.7 H Numbers and Assessed Entropy ................................................ 121

    8.7.1 $H_{original}$ ............................................................................. 122

    8.7.2 $H_{bitstring}$ ............................................................................ 122

    8.7.3 $H_{initial}$ ............................................................................... 122

    8.7.4 $H_r$, $H_c$ ................................................................................ 122

8.7.5 Assessed Entropy ............................................................................... 123

8.7.6 Choosing H Numbers and Setting Test Thresholds ................................ 123

8.8 Collecting Noise Source Data ................................................................... 124

8.9 File Formats for Noise Source Data .......................................................... 126

8.10 Skipping Initial Data .............................................................................. 127

8.11 Software Tools for Processing Noise Source Data .................................... 128

8.11.1 hexbinhex ........................................................................................ 128

8.11.2 hex2bin ............................................................................................ 129

8.11.3 bin2hex ............................................................................................ 129

8.11.4 bin2nistoddball ................................................................................. 130

8.11.5 nistoddball2bin ................................................................................. 130

8.11.6 Restart_slicer ................................................................................... 131

8.11.7 NIST ea_non_iid, ea_iid, restart ........................................................ 133

8.11.8 ea_conditioning ................................................................................ 136

8.11.9 ea_iid ............................................................................................... 141

8.11.10 ea_non_iid ...................................................................................... 143

8.11.11 ea_restart ....................................................................................... 146

8.11.12 ea_transpose ................................................................................... 148

8.11.13 djent ............................................................................................... 149

8.11.14 djenrandom ..................................................................................... 154

8.12 Entropy Assessment Summary ............................................................... 160

**Chapter 9: Entropy Source Validation Certification** ............................... **161**

9.1 CST Labs and Prerequisites ..................................................................... 162

9.2 ESV Certification Activities ...................................................................... 163

9.3 Noise Source Characterization ................................................................. 163

9.4 Physical vs. Nonphysical Noise Sources ................................................... 163

9.5 IID vs. Non-IID Sources ........................................................................... 164

9.6 Entropy Rate Claims and Non-IID Testing ................................................. 165

9.7 Symbol Size Reduction ............................................................................ 165

9.8 Restart Testing ....................................................................................... 169

9.9 Skipping Initial Symbols ........................................................................... 170

9.10 Conditioning Chain Analysis .................................................................. 170

9.11 Entropy Calculations for a Vetted Conditioning Component ................. 171

9.12 Entropy Calculations for a Non-vetted Conditioning Component .......... 175

9.13 Choosing a Conditioner .......................................................................... 176

9.14 SP800-90B Compliance Report .............................................................. 177

9.15 Public Use Document .............................................................................. 179

9.16 Parameter Summary Table ..................................................................... 179

9.17 Continuous Health Tests ........................................................................ 181

9.18 Developer-Defined Continuous Health Tests ......................................... 184

9.19 Example ESV Certificates ....................................................................... 187

9.20 Multiple Operating Environments ......................................................... 187

**Chapter 10: FIPS and Documentation ...................................................... 189**

10.1 FIPS 140-3 PUB ...................................................................................... 189

10.2 Implementation Guidance (IG) ............................................................... 190

10.3 Management Manual (MM) ..................................................................... 190

10.4 CAVP Documents .................................................................................... 191

10.4.1 Block Ciphers and Modes .............................................................. 191

10.4.2 Digital Signatures ......................................................................... 192

10.4.3 Key Derivation Functions .............................................................. 192

10.4.4 Key Management ........................................................................... 192

10.4.5 Message Authentication ............................................................... 193

10.4.6 Random Number Generation ........................................................ 193

10.4.7 Secure Hashing ............................................................................ 193

10.5 Security Policy ........................................................................................ 193

10.6 Entropy Source Validation Public Use Document (ESV PUD) ............... 194

10.7 Entropy Assessment Report (EAR) ........................................................ 194

10.8 Post-Quantum Computing (PQC) Standards ......................................... 194

**Chapter 11: Engaging with a CST Lab.............................................195**

11.1 What Is a Cryptographic Security Testing Lab (CST Lab)?.................... 195

11.2 What CST Lab Services Are Typically Offered?............................... 196

    11.2.1 FIPS 140-3 Consultation and Training ................................ 197

    11.2.2 Generation of CAVP and ESV Certificates ............................ 198

    11.2.3 Request for Guidance ............................................... 198

    11.2.4 Submission Type for Cryptographic Module Certification............. 199

11.3 FIPS Module Life Cycle Timeline ........................................... 201

    11.3.1 "In Review" and "Coordination" ..................................... 203

11.4 When Should a CST Lab Get Involved?........................................ 204

11.5 Strategy for Picking a CST Lab ............................................ 204

11.6 CMVP, ICMC, and CMUF ...................................................... 205

**Index...........................................................................207**

# About the Authors

**David Johnston** is an engineer at Intel working on cryptographic hardware used in Intel CPUs and other silicon products. He has been directly involved in the development of the SP800-90 and FIPS 140 standard revisions and is active in FIPS-related industry forums – he has several FIPS and CAVP certifications. David spent 30 years in various hardware and software roles and is the author of *Random Number Generators—Principles and Practices*.

**Richard Fant** performs security assessments for Intel products and platforms by evaluating the FIPS 140-3 compliance and design strategy for the FPGA Business Unit (Programmable Solutions Group). He also helps lead the Intel FIPS CoE (Center of Excellence) across other Intel business units. Richard has two bachelor's degrees from the University of Texas (Computer Science and Mathematics) as well as a master's degree in Cybersecurity from Syracuse University. He has worked in the semiconductor industry for 20+ years for companies such as Motorola, AMD, and Intel. He also worked at Atsec Information Security performing FIPS evaluations for various semiconductor manufacturers.

# Acknowledgments

Writing a design book on a new version of an evolving standard is very difficult but also rewarding. It is akin to hitting a moving target. More than once we've had to revise and modify earlier chapters of this book as the FIPS 140-3 and ISO 19790 standards matured.

This book would not have been possible without the invaluable assistance given by members of the FIPS Cryptographic Module User Forum (CMUF) in its writing. From providing technical reviews to giving advice on grammar to sharing their FIPS insights and experiences, we'd specifically like to acknowledge Dr. Yi Mao, Thomas Bowen, Kelvin Desplanque, John Kelsey, Stephan Mueller, and Xiaoyu Ruan.

David Johnston

Richard Fant

# Introduction

As long as cryptography has been around, there have been attackers trying to read encrypted messages. Egyptians used simple symbol substitution around 1900 BCE to obscure and modify hieroglyphic text. Approximately 2000 years later, Julius Caesar was using a substitution cipher to pass encrypted messages on the battlefield. Jump forward another 2000 years, and the Germans are using Enigma technology in their war effort. Now, less than 100 years later, quantum computers are allowing attackers an unprecedented decryption ability to read previously secure cryptographic messages.

The competence of modern-day cryptographic attackers can range from a single malicious high-school student to a nation-state bent on world domination and, of course, everything in between. Similarly, the tools of the attacker vary from razor blades used for delidding a CPU to a focused ion beam (FIB) used with an electron microscope to a quantum computer capable of brute-force calculations, allowing it to decipher in days a message that would take a supercomputer more time than the lifespan of the universe to solve.

Historically, the designers of cryptographic algorithms would keep secret exactly how their algorithm worked in encrypting messages. The thinking was that if an attacker didn't know how a message was encrypted, it would be considerably more difficult for unintended recipients to decrypt it. That mindset has changed over the years. A common strategy now is to publicly announce new cryptographic algorithm designs and invite the public to try and break them, for example, new cryptographic algorithm designs are publicly solicited, peer reviewed, openly tested, and possibly adopted after several rounds of evaluation. In fact, the US government has followed this strategy for many post-quantum cryptographically secure (PQC) algorithms before adopting those PQC designs as part of an evolving standard.

That's where this book comes in. FIPS 140 (Federal Information Processing Standards) is the US government computer security standard that specifies requirements for cryptographic modules. The target audience for this book is any engineer working on cryptographic products intended for use by the US or Canadian governments.

The book also covers FIPS topics from multiple perspectives: the cryptographic product designer/vendor, the external Cryptographic and Security Testing (CST) Labs, and the government regulatory bodies such as the National Institute of Standards and Technology (NIST) and the Canadian Centre for Cyber Security (CCCS).

This book is intended as a reference guide, and so for the convenience of the reader, some topics and definitions are repeated multiple times throughout; the idea being that each section/chapter should not necessarily require the reader to review preceding chapters as a prerequisite for understanding the current section.

**CHAPTER 1**

# Introduction to FIPS and CMVP

## 1.1  What Is FIPS 140-3?

FIPS 140-3 (Federal Information Processing Standards) is the US government computer security standard that specifies requirements for cryptographic modules. If a US government agency wishes to purchase a cryptographic product, then that product must be FIPS certified. In recent years, FIPS has become a popular requirement in the financial and health care sectors as well. The first FIPS certificate for a cryptographic module was officially released in 1995. However, during the first 20+ years of the FIPS program, many cryptographic products sold to the US government by vendors were routinely granted special waivers which allowed the product to be non-FIPS compliant for various reasons. This vendor strategy changed in 2021.

In May 2021, US President Joe Biden signed Cybersecurity Executive Order 14028.[1] At its core, the Executive Order essentially stated that waivers would no longer be granted for cybersecurity compliance. This new position was taken in response to incidents such as the ransomware attack on the Colonial Pipeline and supply-chain attacks on SolarWinds. The Executive Order mandated that federal agencies adopt new measures to increase the cybersecurity of the United States while reducing its attack surface. One such federal agency affected by this mandate was the National Institute of Standards and Technology (NIST) and its Cryptographic Module Validation Program.

---

[1] www.nist.gov/itl/executive-order-14028-improving-nations-cybersecurity

© David Johnston and Richard Fant 2024
D. Johnston and R. Fant, *Designing to FIPS-140*, https://doi.org/10.1007/979-8-8688-0125-9_1

THE WHITE HOUSE

BRIEFING ROOM

### Executive Order on Improving the Nation's Cybersecurity

MAY 12, 2021 • PRESIDENTIAL ACTIONS

By the authority vested in me as President by the Constitution and the laws of the United States of America, it is hereby ordered as follows:

Section 1. Policy. The United States faces persistent and increasingly sophisticated malicious cyber campaigns that threaten the public sector, the private sector, and ultimately the American people's security and privacy. The Federal Government must improve its efforts to identify, deter, protect against, detect, and respond to these actions and actors. The Federal Government must also carefully examine what occurred during any major cyber incident and apply lessons learned. But

The Cryptographic Module Validation Program (CMVP) is a joint venture between the governments of the United States and Canada which defines and validates the security accreditation programs for cryptographic modules. These standards are known collectively as FIPS. As shown in Table 1-1, the first standard was used in 1994 and the most recent one in 2020. There is also an overlap when the newest FIPS standard and its predecessor are both valid.

***Table 1-1.*** *FIPS Standard Lifespans*

| FIPS Standard | Testing-Allowed Start Date | Sunset Date |
|---|---|---|
| 140-1 | January 1994 | May 2002 |
| 140-2 | November 2001 | September 2021 |
| 140-3 | September 2020 | No date defined |

Please note that FIPS 140-2 was valid for almost 20 years and had reached a fairly mature and stable state. This is not the case for FIPS 140-3. At the time of this writing, there are many incomplete sections of the FIPS 140-3 standards. Many of the use cases, requirements, and interpretations of FIPS 140-2 will eventually migrate to FIPS

140-3, but some of them won't. The FIPS 140-3 standards are based on ISO 19790:2012. Sections of the FIPS standards which expand on the ISO standards are generally documented in the FIPS 140-3 Implementation Guidance (frequently referred to as the "IG").

This book is our "best guess" based on decades of FIPS experience and close involvement with the CMVP reviewers and user forums. This book is intended for design engineers and architects who need a FIPS-compliant product; however, program managers will find some useful information with regard to planning their road maps for FIPS products. It is important to bear in mind that certifying a module as FIPS compliant is more of a marathon than a sprint.

Throughout this book, the reader will see numerous instances of the terms "**shall**" or "**shall not**." These are terms with very specific meaning in all the FIPS standards. "**Shall**" means that the statement associated with it is mandatory and must be followed. "**Shall not**" means the statement associated with it is not allowed under any circumstances.

# 1.2  The Major Tasks in FIPS Design

The FIPS standards define five module types and four security levels. Once you've determined what these will be for your product, then achieving FIPS compliance can be broken down into four main categories. These categories are explored at greater length later in this book:

- Collaboration with a Third-Party CST Lab

- Entropy Assessment

- Cryptographic Algorithm Validation Program

- Pitfalls to Avoid

## 1.2.1  FIPS Module Definitions

A FIPS module is the entity that is certified when claiming compliance with the FIPS 140-3 requirements. A module can take many forms. For example, a USB device, a software application, a PCI card, a PC, a rack mounted server, and a subcircuit in a silicon chip are entities that could be FIPS certified, providing their physical properties, firmware, and software meet the FIPS 140-3 requirements.

In addition, every module has a logical cryptographic boundary, commonly called the FIPS boundary. For FIPS hardware modules, there must also be a defined physical boundary. The logical and physical boundaries may be the same, or they may be different. The functional parts of the FIPS module are inside the logical cryptographic boundary. The FIPS 140-3 standard defines rules for how data and control pass through this boundary. The FIPS boundary is around everything in the module, which includes cryptographic components along with everything else involved in a computing device. This FIPS boundary might be defined as the chassis of the device, the package of the chip, or a logical boundary around a software module. Whatever it is called, in this book we will stick with "cryptographic boundary" or "crypto boundary" to match ISO 19790:2012.

Defining the FIPS cryptographic boundary is the most critical step in determining the scope of FIPS compliance. This is an important consideration since one strategy attempted by vendors over the years is to design products with a minimum cryptographic footprint requiring the least amount of design effort in order to claim FIPS compliance. Their justification is that since the product now has a "FIPS Certified" component, this allows the product to be sold to federal agencies. This was a successful marketing strategy for many years; however, most end customers (and the CMVP) eventually became aware of this tactic and are now very strict on what the vendor claims as their cryptographic boundary. For example, carrying a FIPS certified smart phone in your pocket while driving your car does not mean that your car is also FIPS certified.

What gives the crypto boundary meaning is the set of rules about how data and control can pass through it. These rules are described in terms of logical and physical ports on the boundary – physical ports being actual electrical connectors and LEDs or, in the case of a software module, API calls. The logical interfaces run over the physical interfaces, and the logical interfaces fall into one of the four buckets:

- Data input
- Data output
- Status output
- Control input

There are five module types defined in the FIPS 140-3 standards.[2] Later in this chapter, you'll find URLs showing actual real-world examples of these different module types. The Security Policy for each example contains diagrams that better illustrate how

---

[2] ISO 19790:2012 Section 7.2.2

to differentiate between the module types and their cryptographic boundaries. The following examples are not exhaustive but rather give an idea of the module types and boundaries available. There are many more boundary and subcomponent permutations that would satisfy the FIPS module type definitions.

## 1.2.2  Hardware Module

A hardware module primarily contains non-modifiable or immutable components. Software, firmware, or even operating system (O/S) components may be included within the cryptographic boundary. The cryptographic boundary must be specified at a physical hardware perimeter. Once this hardware module is certified as FIPS compliant, any change to its design will require revalidation for FIPS compliance. Examples of a non-modifiable operational environment (OE) include firmware contained in ROM or software contained in a computer with the I/O devices disabled.

In Figure 1-1, the dashed lines represent the FIPS module's cryptographic boundary. The dashed line is also the physical boundary. This is an example where the cryptographic boundary and the hardware boundary are the same. The outermost shaded square is its non-modifiable operational environment (OE). As paraphrased from FIPS 140-3: "a *non-modifiable operational environment is designed to prevent modification to the module components, the computing platform, or the operating system.*"

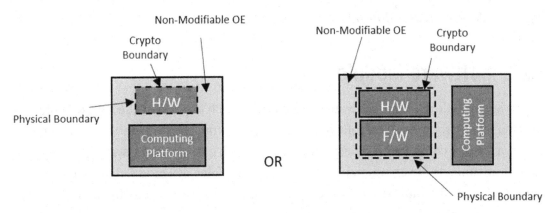

***Figure 1-1.***  *Hardware Module (Left), Hardware-Firmware Hybrid Module (Right)*

Now we will logically map the generic block diagram from Figure 1-1 to a real-world example in Figure 1-2: Intel's Offload and Crypto Subsystem (OCS). This is a FIPS 140-2 Certified Module (Cert# 4025) and is defined as a Security Level 2 hardware module with immutable firmware contained within its logical cryptographic boundary. The OCS ROM code is actually implemented as part of the silicon substrate and so is non-modifiable unless the chip is physically damaged. As stated before, if any of the components or version numbers within this OE are changed, then the entire module must be recertified. For example, changing the computing platform from Lakemont v3.7 to v3.8 is considered a modification and would invalidate this module. The module's Security Policy with more details can be found here: `https://csrc.nist.gov/projects/cryptographic-module-validation-program/certificate/4025`. Please note that for simplicity, Figure 1-2 does not show every individual component as diagrammed in the Security Policy. Rather, it just shows the major IP blocks with boundaries.

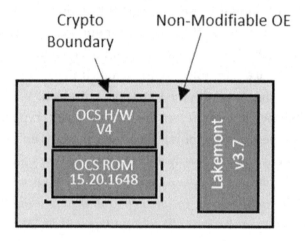

***Figure 1-2.***  *Hardware Module*

## 1.2.3  Software Module

A software module contains software components which execute inside a modifiable operational environment. The software component(s) must be executable code which does not require compilation. The computing platform and operating system of the module are outside the cryptographic boundary. Examples of a modifiable OE could be a PC's O/S, a configurable smart card O/S, or programmable firmware. In Figure 1-3, the dashed lines represent the module's cryptographic boundary. The outermost shaded square is its modifiable operational environment. As paraphrased from FIPS 140-3: "a *modifiable operational environment is designed to accept functional changes that may contain untrusted software. It may be reconfigured to add/delete/modify functionality, and/or may include general-purpose operating system capabilities."*

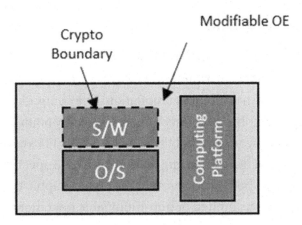

***Figure 1-3.*** *Software Figure Module*

Here, we map the generic block diagram from Figure 1-3 to a real-world example in Figure 1-4. This is a FIPS 140-2 Certified Module (Cert #4132) which is defined as a Security Level 1 software module with a modifiable OE. Note that the cryptographic boundary includes crypto software for both the Linux user space and the Linux kernel space. A key point here is that the cryptographic boundary is a *logical* boundary, not a *physical* one. In general, this means that as long as the crypto boundary is wholly contained within the physical boundary, the crypto boundary can cross both hardware and software components or, as in this example, even logically divide a software stack. This module's Security Policy with more details can be found here: `https://csrc.nist.gov/projects/` `cryptographic-module-validation-program/certificate/4132`. Please note that for simplicity, Figure 1-4 does not show every individual component as diagrammed in the Security Policy. Rather, it just shows the major IP blocks with boundaries.

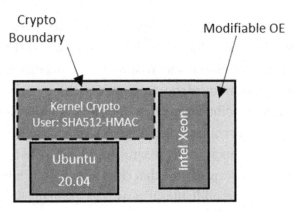

***Figure 1-4.*** *Software Module*

# 1.2.4 Firmware Module

A firmware module contains firmware components which execute in either a limited or non-modifiable operational environment. The firmware component(s) must be executable code which does not require compilation. The computing platform and O/S are external to the cryptographic boundary but are "explicitly bound" to the firmware module. This explicit binding means that the module is only FIPS certified to work with the version numbers of the computing platform and O/S specified in its Security Policy. In Figure 1-5, the dashed lines represent the cryptographic boundary. The outermost shaded square is its limited or non-modifiable operational environment. The definition of a non-modifiable environment is given in the "Hardware Module" section. But a limited operational environment as paraphrased from FIPS 140-3 is "*designed to allow controlled modification by an operator or process to the module components, the computing platform, or the operating system.*"

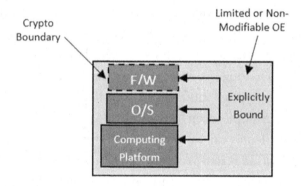

***Figure 1-5.***  *Firmware Module*

Figure 1-6 shows the mapping from the generic block diagram from Figure 1-5 to a real-world example. This is a FIPS 140-2 Certified Module (Cert #4173) which is defined as a Security Level 1 firmware module operating within a non-modifiable operational environment. This means that none of the components within its cryptographic boundary or the OE can be modified. Note that the cryptographic module also has explicit version numbers of the computing platform and O/S explicitly associated with it. If any of those components change, then the entire module would have to be revalidated.

In this example, it is interesting to note that changes are not allowed based on two different conditions: it's a non-modifiable OE as well as explicitly bound to specific version numbers. Its Security Policy with more details can be found here: https://csrc. nist.gov/projects/cryptographic-module-validation-program/certificate/4173.

Please note that for simplicity, Figure 1-5 does not show every individual component as diagrammed in the Security Policy. Rather, it just shows the major IP blocks with boundaries.

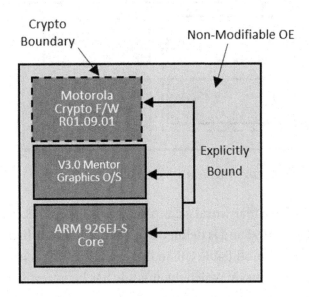

***Figure 1-6.***  *Firmware Module*

## 1.2.5 Software-Hardware Hybrid Module

A *software-hardware hybrid* module contains both software and hardware components, but the software components are disjoint from the hardware component. The software component(s) must be executable code which does not require compilation. The computing platform and O/S are external to the cryptographic boundary. The hardware component can contain embedded software. In Figure 1-7, the dashed lines represent the module's cryptographic boundary. The outermost shaded square is its modifiable operational environment.

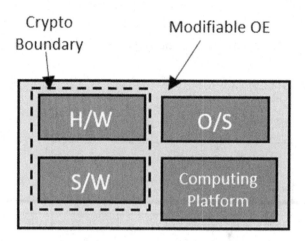

***Figure 1-7.*** *Hybrid Software Module*

Mapping Figure 1-7 to a real-world example gives us Figure 1-8. This is a FIPS 140-2 Certified Module (Cert# 4109) and is defined as a Security Level 1 hybrid software module operating within a modifiable OE. In this example, the Security Policy lists six different computing platforms on which the module has been certified. If the end user chooses to use a computing platform not contained in that list, then the CMVP makes no claims on whether the module will operate correctly. The module's Security Policy with more details can be found here: `https://csrc.nist.gov/projects/cryptographic-module-validation-program/certificate/4109`. Please note that for simplicity, Figure 1-8 does not show every individual component as diagrammed in the Security Policy. Rather, it just shows the major IP blocks with boundaries.

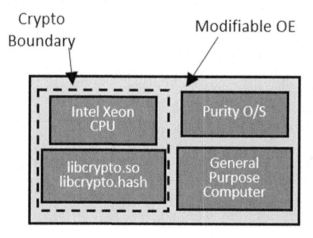

***Figure 1-8.*** *Hybrid Software Module*

# 1.2.6 Firmware-Hardware Hybrid Module

A *firmware-hardware hybrid* module contains both firmware and hardware components, but the hardware component is disjoint from the firmware component. This means the firmware is not contained within the hardware, but both are still within the cryptographic boundary. Also, the computing platform and O/S are external to the cryptographic boundary but are "explicitly bound" to the hybrid firmware module. This explicit binding means that the module is only FIPS certified to work with the specific version numbers of the computing platform and O/S. In Figure 1-9, the dashed lines represent the cryptographic boundary. The outermost shaded square is its operational environment.

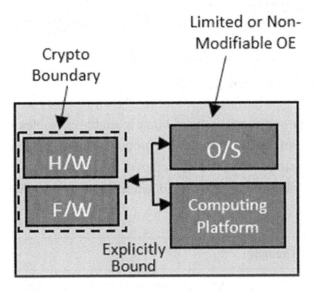

***Figure 1-9.*** *Hybrid Firmware Module*

In Figure 1-9, we show a real-world example as depicted in Figure 1-8. This is a FIPS 140-2 Security Level 1 hybrid firmware module (Cert #4150) based on Intel's Tiger Lake. The module operates in a limited operational environment. The operator cannot modify the firmware component of the module contained within the module's cryptographic boundary. Notice that the cryptographic module within the dashed line is explicitly bound to a specific version of the operating system (15.0.20.1648) and a specific version of the computing platform (Lakemont v3.7). These cannot be changed without revalidating the entire module. Its Security Policy with more details can be found here: https://csrc.nist.gov/projects/cryptographic-module-validation-program/certificate/4150. Please note that for simplicity, Figure 1-10 does not show every individual component as diagrammed in the Security Policy. Rather, it just shows the major IP blocks with boundaries.

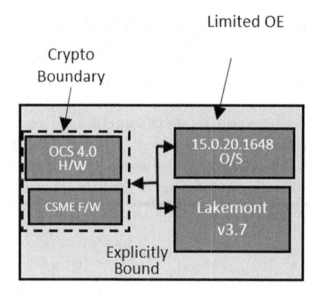

**Figure 1-10.**  *Hybrid Firmware Module*

The following table summarizes the publicly available examples shown earlier, which are available from the CMVP validated module website. You can also search for additional examples using the "Search" function of the website if none of the examples included here match what you are looking for since there are over 4000 validated modules listed there.

| Module Type | CMVP Example |
|---|---|
| Hardware | https://csrc.nist.gov/projects/cryptographic-module-validation-program/certificate/4025 |
| Software | https://csrc.nist.gov/projects/cryptographic-module-validation-program/certificate/4070 |
| Firmware | https://csrc.nist.gov/projects/cryptographic-module-validation-program/certificate/4173 |
| Software Hybrid | https://csrc.nist.gov/projects/cryptographic-module-validation-program/certificate/4109 |
| Firmware Hybrid | https://csrc.nist.gov/projects/cryptographic-module-validation-program/certificate/4150 |

## 1.2.7  Firmware vs. Software

Frequently, FIPS 140-3 will give specific definitions for commonly used terms. For example, FIPS 140-3 makes the following distinctions between firmware and software within a cryptographic module:

> *Firmware*: Code executed in a non-modifiable or limited operational environment and stored in hardware within the cryptographic boundary and which cannot be dynamically written or modified during execution

> *Software*: Code executed in a modifiable operation environment and stored on erasable media and which can be dynamically written and modified during execution

One important note here is that firmware and software must be in an executable format since FIPS 140-3 doesn't allow source code or "just-in-time" compilation within the cryptographic module.

## 1.2.8  Security-Level Definitions

FIPS modules are also assigned a security level ranging from 1 to 4.[3] Security Level 1 consists of requirements that are relatively simple to implement, while Security Level 4 modules are much more difficult to design and validate. In general, as the security levels increase, the FIPS standards require increasingly more robust and rigorous requirements to protect the Sensitive Security Parameters (SSP) as well as the components and operations within the cryptographic module. In addition, all FIPS requirements in the 11 Core Security Areas are applied differently depending on which security level is claimed for the module. Table 1-2 is derived from the FIPS 140-3 standards[4] and shows a summary of how the different security levels map to different requirements. Please note this table is not comprehensive. There are additional requirements not shown here.

---

[3] ISO 19790:2012, Section 5
[4] ISO 19790:2012, Section 7.1, Table 1.1

***Table 1-2.*** *FIPS Security Requirements*

| Area | Security Topic | Security Level 1 | Security Level 2 | Security Level 3 | Security Level 4 |
|------|----------------|------------------|------------------|------------------|------------------|
| 1 | Cryptographic Module Specification | Specification of cryptographic module, cryptographic boundary, approved security functions, and normal and degraded modes of operation. Description of cryptographic module, including all hardware, software, and firmware components. All services provide status information to indicate when the service utilizes an approved cryptographic algorithm, security function, or process in an approved manner | | | |
| 2 | Cryptographic Module Interfaces | Required and optional interfaces. Specification of all interfaces and of all input and output data paths | | Trusted Channel with identity-based authentication. "In-Use" indicator required | [All SL3 req.] + Trusted Channel using multi-factor identity-based authentication |
| 3 | Roles, Services, and Authentication | Logical separation of required and optional roles and services. This separation can be satisfied in documentation. No authentication required | Role-based or identity-based operator authentication | Identity-based operator authentication | Multifactor authentication |
| | | Crypto officer role required. User role and maintenance role optional. Need a service that outputs module version information | | | |
| 4 | Software/ Firmware Security | Integrity test: [HASH, HMAC, Digital Signature, EDC]. Module Interfaces defined | Integrity test: [HMAC, Digital Signature, EDC]. Only executable code allowed (e.g., no src code) | Integrity test: [Digital Signature, EDC]. Only executable code allowed | |
| | | EDC integrity test for firmware within a h/w module or disjoint h/w component of hybrid module | | | |
| 5 | Operational Environment (OE) | Non-modifiable, limited or modifiable. Module controls SSPs | Modifiable. Role-based or discretionary access control. Audit mechanism | No additional requirements | |
| 6 | Physical Security **(Hardware, Firmware, or Hybrid Modules Only)** | Production-grade components. If maintenance mode supported, then procedural or automatic zeroization required when accessing it | Tamper evidence. Opaque covering or enclosure. Prevent direct observation through holes and slits | Tamper detection and response. Tamper evident seals uniquely identified. Strong enclosure or coating. Protection from direct probing. EFP **or** EFT. If maintenance mode supported, then automatic and immediate zeroization when accessing it | Tamper detection and response envelope. Tamper evident seals uniquely identified. For multi-chips, tamper response requires automatic and immediate zeroization. EFP required. Fault injection mitigation |
| | | Need a defined physical boundary of module | | | |

*(continued)*

*Table 1-2.* (*continued*)

| Area | Security Topic | | Security Level 1 | Security Level 2 | Security Level 3 | Security Level 4 |
|------|----------------|---|------------------|------------------|------------------|------------------|
| 7 | Noninvasive Security | | Not applicable if module is not designed to mitigate against noninvasive attacks | | | |
| | | | Documentation and effectiveness of mitigation techniques specified in ISO 19790:2012 Annex F | | [All SL1 and SL2 reqs.] + Noninvasive attack mitigation testing | |
| 8 | Sensitive Security Parameters (SSP) Management | | Manually established SSPs may be entered or outputted in plaintext form | | Manually established SSPs may be entered or outputted in either encrypted form, via a trusted channel or using split knowledge procedures | |
| | | | Define management of random bit generators (RBG), SSP generation, establishment, entry and output, storage, and zeroization. RBG state info, hash value of passwords are CSPs. Automated SSP transport or SSP agreement using approved methods | | | |
| | | | SSP Zeroization: May be done procedurally in Security Policy | SSP Zeroization: Status indicator required upon completion | SSP Zeroization: Status indicator required | SSP Zeroization: Status indicator required. Zeroization of *ALL* SSPs returns module to factory state |
| 9 | Self-Tests | | No additional requirements | | Maintain error logs of most recent errors. Module must perform automatic periodic self-tests | |
| | | | No data or control output allowed when module is in error state | | | |
| | | | Preoperational Self -Tests (POST): Software/firmware integrity, bypass, and critical functions test (if applicable) | | | |
| | | | Conditional Self-Test: Cryptographic algorithm self-test (CAST), pair-wise consistency, software/firmware loading, manual entry, conditional bypass (if applicable), and critical functions test (if applicable) | | | |
| | | | Hardware modules with no software/firmware must implement at least one cryptographic algorithm self-test | | | |
| 10 | Life Cycle Assurance | Configuration Management | Configuration management system for cryptographic module, components, and documentation. Each uniquely identified and tracked throughout lifecycle | | Automated configuration management system | |
| | | Design | Module designed to allow testing of all provided security-related services | | | |
| | | FSM | Finite state model. Each distinct cryptographic module service, security function use, error state, self-test, or operator authentication **shall** be depicted as a separate state | | | |
| | | Development | Annotated source code, schematics, or HDL. For example, inline comments | [All SL1 req.] + Software high-level language. Hardware high-level descriptive language | | [All SL1,2,3 req.] + Documentation annotated with preconditions upon entry into module components and post-conditions expected to be "true" when components are completed |

(*continued*)

***Table 1-2.*** (*continued*)

| Area | Security Topic | | Security Level 1 | Security Level 2 | Security Level 3 | Security Level 4 |
|------|------|------|------|------|------|------|
| | | Testing | Documentation specifies the vendor's positive and negative functional testin | [All SL1,2] + Documentation specifies the vendor's low-level testing | | |
| | | | Automated security diagnostics tools required for software, firmware, and hybrid modules | | | |
| | | Delivery and Operation | Installation initialization, and startup procedures | Delivery procedures | | [All SL1,2,3] + Operator authentication using vendor-provided authentication information |
| | | | No additional requirements | Documentation specifies procedures for tamper detection during delivery | | |
| | | End Of Life | Documentation specifies the procedures for secure sanitization of the module to remove sensitive information (e.g., SSPs, user data, etc.) | | [All SL1,2] + Documentation specifies the procedures for the secure destruction of the module | |
| | | Guidance | Administrator and non-administrator guidance | | | |
| 11 | Mitigation of Other Attacks | | Specification of mitigation of attacks for which no testable requirements are currently available | | | [All SL1,2,3] + Specification of mitigation of attacks with testable requirements |

# 1.3  FIPS Pitfalls to Avoid

Designing a product to be FIPS compliant has always been challenging. FIPS 140-2 was the standard for almost 20 years. By the time FIPS 140-2 was deprecated, it was a fairly stable set of rules and guidelines with thousands of examples of successfully validated FIPS 140-2 modules. By contrast, FIPS 140-3 is very new and is still experiencing growing pains as its documentation is updated and refreshed. This changing landscape adds a new level of difficulty for FIPS designers.

As you might expect, there are initial decisions that must be made early in the design process that have an enormous ripple effect on the final FIPS design. In addition, there are numerous FIPS documents which must be consulted. Many of these documents are cross-referenced to yet other documents. Some of these documents change often since FIPS 140-3 is still changing. While it is challenging to keep current on the latest FIPS requirements, there are some recurring pitfalls that seem to be consistent despite the constant flux.

This section will attempt to highlight some of these most common mistakes made by FIPS designers. While this is not a comprehensive list, it does reflect anecdotal experience from the authors.

## 1.3.1 Documentation

By far, the most common design mistakes are due to "stale" FIPS documentation. Before finalizing upon any critical design decisions, make sure your designers have the latest version of whatever specification they are designed against. Also, check when the next version of that specification is due to be published. If the next publication date is soon, you might consider adopting the draft release of the next specification in your design.

Fortunately, the CMVP is proactive in releasing draft versions of standards for public comment before their official release. While it can be a reasonable strategy for a designer to align their module with a pending release, there is obviously a risk if the draft changes. The best way to keep track of the likelihood of future updates and their release dates is to join the CMUF described in Chapter 11.

# 1.4 Most Common Pitfalls

Table 1-3 highlights some of the higher-level pitfalls suitable for executive-level consumption. These are fairly basic, but even experienced FIPS designers will on occasion miss them.

***Table 1-3.*** *Most Common Pitfalls*

| Pitfall | FIPS 140-3 Strategy |
|---|---|
| FIPS crypto boundary | Define the FIPS boundary as small as possible so it just contains the component(s) which implements the crypto functions, such as a SW crypto library or HW crypto engine. The larger your FIPS boundary, the more work your FIPS designers may have. Also, define the "User" entity carefully; is the "User" a person, a firmware image, an external process, etc. |
| TRNG entropy capture | The TRNG must have an interface for an external test tool to extract raw noise source output. The interface may be available only in debug/maintenance mode |
| Theory of least privilege | Access to functions, variables, and registers must apply the theory of least privilege. For example, key program registers shall be write-only and not readable |
| Zeroization service | Zeroize volatile keys (secret keys, private keys, and public keys) when no longer needed. For example, zeroize local and heap variables before function return |
| Authentication | For Security Levels 2–4, implement identity-based operator authentication. Even though role-based authentication is allowed at Level 2, a better strategy is to upgrade to identity based |
| Module ID and version numbers | Implement a service where a user can read the module's model name, module ID, versions, etc. |
| FIPS mode indicator | Every crypto service provided by the module must indicate if this service is FIPS compliant, i.e., using only FIPS-approved algorithms |
| Physical security | For HW and hybrid modules only: The physical boundary must meet certain requirements including physical security testing by a CST Lab |
| Testing attack mitigation | If a vendor publicly claims that their module has implemented mitigation of certain attacks, then the CST Lab must test those claims. If a vendor has implemented such attack mitigation, but doesn't claim it publicly, this testing is not required |

Table 1-4 highlights the pitfalls related to the cryptographic algorithms contained within the FIPS module.

*Table 1-4.* *Cryptographic Algorithm Pitfalls*

| Pitfall | FIPS 140-3 Strategy |
|---|---|
| FIPS algorithms | Where possible, try to use only FIPS-approved crypto algorithms (including key derivation). While it is possible to have non-approved FIPS algorithms, it does require some extra work in the documentation |
| Self-test | Every implementation of every FIPS-approved crypto algorithm must pass a known-answer-test (KAT) before its first use. This KAT can be done at power-on or at any time prior to using that algorithm for the first time |
| Integrity self-test | Implement an integrity self-test at boot for any software/firmware components. This integrity test is required before the SW or FW can be executed |
| Pairwise self-test | Keypairs for Elliptic Curve Digital Signature Algorithm (ECDSA) or RSA which are generated from a random bit generator (RBG) must use a pairwise consistency self-test before use |
| Algorithm testing interfaces | Every implementation of every FIPS-approved crypto algorithm should have an interface for external test tools to supply input test vectors and read out output response vectors. The interface may be available only in debug/maintenance mode |
| GCM encrypt key + IV | For Galois Counter Mode (GCM) encrypt, the module itself must generate key and/or IV randomly (i.e., key and IV cannot both be input into module) |
| XTS key1 + key2 | For XTS, the module must make sure key1 != key2, before performing encryption or decryption |

# 1.5 Glossary/Abbreviations

| | |
|---|---|
| ACVP | Automated Cryptographic Validation Protocol. This is the hand-shaking protocol between the CMVP servers and the accredited CST Labs. Used for algorithm validation |
| ACVTS | Automated Cryptographic Validation Test System. Used in the CAVP to validate algorithms |
| CAVP | Cryptographic Algorithm Validation Program. Used to validate algorithms. Not to be confused with the CMVP. CAVP is a prerequisite of CMVP |
| CMVP | Cryptographic Module Validation Program. Used to validate cryptographic modules. Not to be confused with the CAVP |
| Cryptographic Service | These are services contained within a FIPS validated module. For example, a cryptographic algorithm such as AES-GCM is a cryptographic service. Functions like zeroization or "get version number," while not cryptographic algorithms, are still cryptographic services |
| CSP | Critical Security Parameters, e.g., private keys |
| EDC-16 | Error Detection Code which uses 16 bits |
| EFP | Environmental Failure Protection. Protects against a compromise of the security of a cryptographic module due to environmental conditions outside of the module's normal operating range |
| EFT | Environmental Failure Testing |
| ESV or Entropy Source Validation | This is a CMVP program which validates a vendor's design related to entropy generation and manipulation. This is a prerequisite for CMVP validation |
| IG or Implementation Guidance | This is a CMVP publication which provides detailed guidance on FIPS implementations |
| OE | Operational environment in which the module executes. Can be non-modifiable, modifiable, or limited |

*(continued)*

| POST | Preoperational Self-Test. Testing done prior to first use of an algorithm, not necessarily at power-on. Note: For FIPS 140-2, "POST" was defined as Power-On Self-Test, and all algorithms were tested then. For FIPS 140-3, all algorithms just need to be tested before their first use |
|------|------|
| PSP | Public Security Parameters, e.g., public keys |
| RBG | Random Bit Generator |
| SP or Security Policy | This is a non-proprietary and publicly available user manual that describes the security aspect of a validated FIPS module. It will include a list of algorithms supported and all individual certifications needed for the module to be certified |
| SP or Special Publication | These are official publications of NIST. For example, NIST SP 800-140-D is the Special Publication for the 800 series, 140-D, which describes Critical and Public Security Parameters |
| SSP | Sensitive Security Parameters. Consists of PSP (Public Security Parameters) and CSP (Critical Security Parameters) |
| TRNG | True Random Number Generator. This is a nondeterministic random number generator |
| Zeroization | All unprotected SSPs are set to zero. All modules must include a zeroization service |

# CHAPTER 2

# Core Concepts

Here, we drill one level down to look at a number of specific technical concepts and defined terms within FIPS 140 and ISO/IEC 19790:2012.

## 2.1 FIPS 140 Module

A FIPS 140 module is the entity that is certified that it complies with the FIPS 140 standard. A module can take many forms. A USB device, a PCI card, a PC, a rack mounted server, and a subcircuit in a silicon chip are all examples of devices that could be FIPS certified provided that the physical properties, firmware, and software meet the FIPS 140 requirements.

Common FIPS 140 modules include network key management devices, network random number servers, SSL/TLS offload engines, HSMs (hardware security modules), and network routers.

## 2.2 FIPS/Cryptographic Boundary

A module has a boundary, commonly called the "FIPS boundary," but in ISO/IEC 19790:2012 is named the "cryptographic boundary." This is usually both a logical and physical boundary. The functional parts of the FIPS module are inside the boundary, and the FIPS 140 standard defines rules for how information and control pass over the boundary. The term "cryptographic boundary" doesn't really capture the idea of the thing being defined. The boundary is around everything in the module, which includes cryptography along with everything else involved in a computing device. So "module boundary" works better. This boundary might be defined as the case of the device, the package of the chip, or a logical boundary around a software module. Whatever it is called, in this book we will stick with "cryptographic boundary" to match ISO 19790.

© David Johnston and Richard Fant 2024
D. Johnston and R. Fant, *Designing to FIPS-140*, https://doi.org/10.1007/979-8-8688-0125-9_2

What gives the boundary meaning is the set of rules about how data and control can pass through the boundary. This is described in terms of logical and physical ports on the boundary – physical ports being actual electrical connectors and LEDs or, in the case of a software module, API calls. The logical interfaces run over the physical interfaces, and the logical interfaces fall into one of four buckets – data input, data output, status output, and control input.

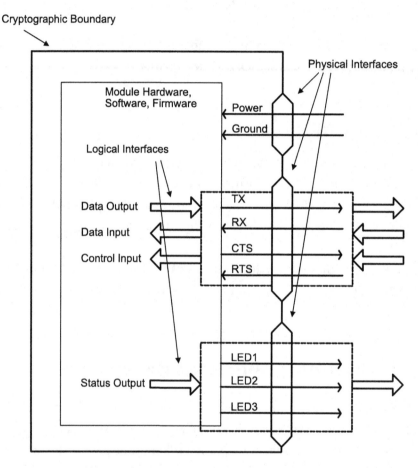

**Figure 2-1.**  *Logical and Physical Ports of a FIPS Module*

In the example in Figure 2-1, a hypothetical hardware module is shown, with the cryptographic boundary and three physical ports – power, serial port, and LED output. The logical interfaces run over the serial port and the LEDs.

The power interface is present but doesn't map cleanly to the logical interface types. In general, the module is going to bring the power interface into the security analysis, for example, failing safe with out-of-spec input on the power lines and preventing information leakage via the power interface such as with DPA (Differential Power Analysis) attacks.

Physical interfaces can take many forms, for example, Ethernet, USB host, USB device, keyboard input, screen output, touch screen input, and RS232 serial ports.

Logical interfaces often operate over TCP/IP or some other higher-level protocol. The need for a trusted channel over the interfaces often leads to the use of TLS security to provide authentication, authorization, and privacy services over the interface. Similarly, a PCI card might run TLS-like protocols over a PCI port, but with inputs and outputs encoded as PCI reads and writes.

# 2.3 SSPs

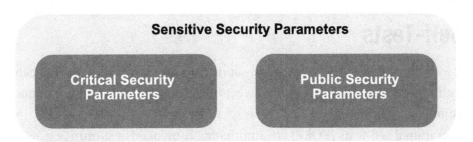

***Figure 2-2.*** *Sensitive Security Parameters*

SSP (Sensitive Security Parameter) is the name of data elements that hold security relevant information. This could be public or private. A private SSP is called CSP (Critical Security Parameter), and a public SSP is called a PSP (Public Security Parameter). Within the module, the SSPs can be stored as either plaintext or in an encrypted format.

CSPs should be protected from being revealed outside the FIPS boundary and from unauthorized alteration. Examples of a CSP include cryptographic keys, hash digests of passwords, RBG seed values, etc.

PSPs should be protected from unauthorized modification. Examples include nonces to be used or an RSA public key. A PSP is deemed protected if it is associated with an integrity value such as a hash digest.

# 2.4  Security Policy

The Security Policy (SP) is a nonproprietary public document that describes a FIPS validated module. The SP must contain a list of all the cryptographic services (including algorithms) contained within the module. Note that not all cryptographic services are algorithms. Consider, for example, a zeroization function which is a cryptographic service but does not have a specific algorithm associated with it. Similarly, a function which returns the cryptographic module software version number is a cryptographic service but not an algorithm. By contrast, a cryptographic algorithm might be a SHA-2 algorithm or even a non-approved cryptographic algorithm such as Rivest Cipher 4 (RC4).

The SP must also describe how the module is initialized the very first time in the field as well as define the different user roles such as crypto officer and user. The SP must describe the Life Cycle Assurance infrastructure used in the module's design such as internal documentation, version control, and even how the validated module is securely delivered to the end user.

# 2.5  Self-Tests

Self-tests as defined in ISO 19790 are stand-alone tests within the module that can be run without external control or input of vectors. As defined, self-tests are either preoperational or conditional.

Preoperational self-tests (POST) are automatically invoked at startup (e.g., power up, reset, reboot, instantiation). The module does not enter the operational state until the preoperational self-tests have completed without error.

Conditional self-tests are run when the defined conditions are met for running, but the conditions for some of the conditional tests include that the test is run preoperationally, so there is overlap between the two classifications.

The test types may all be used as conditional tests but tests 3, 5, and 6 must be implemented as preoperational tests "as applicable," which I take to mean that there is no point in a software or firmware load test if you don't have software or firmware:

1. Cryptographic Algorithm Self-Test

2. Pair-Wise Consistency Test

3. Software/Firmware Load Test

4.  Manual Entry Test

5.  Bypass Test

6.  Critical Function Test

The ISO 19790:2012 standard specifies periodic self-tests, which must be available on demand either through a service interface or restarting the module. For Security Levels 3 and 4, the tests must also be automatically run periodically.

An important difference between FIPS 140-2 and FIPS 140-3 based on ISO/IEC 19790:2012 is that the ISO standard is specific about the response to an error failure, whereas FIPS 140-2 is not.

# 2.6  Zeroization

Zeroization is primarily addressed in Section 7.9.7 of ISO/IEC 19790:2012. A note on spelling: When working with FIPS, one will often see the word "zeroization" used interchangeably with "zeroisation." This is not a typo. The ISO 19790 documentation uses the European spelling with "s," but FIPS 140, written mostly by the US government, uses the American spelling with "z." Both are correct.

In response to detected attacks, a fault condition, an on-demand request, or the de-instantiation of a cryptographic service, the unprotected SSPs and keys must be destroyed. This can be through writing all zeroes or ones to the state elements that hold the SSPs or overwriting with random data. It is required that following the zeroization, the SSPs cannot be recovered. In addition, the zeroization method should also execute quickly enough to prevent an attacker from obtaining any useful information from the SSPs.

The implementation of the self-tests will typically use SSP values that are used exclusively for those tests. These SSPs do not need to be zeroed, but they must not be the SSPs used after the self-test.

FIPS 140-3 allows a vendor to zeroize their FIPS module "procedurally" for modules claiming Security Level 1. This basically means a vendor can use a power cycle of the module to satisfy the zeroization requirement; the only caveat is that the Security Policy of the module must clearly state that power cycling will zeroize the module.

## 2.7  Life Cycle Assurance

Life Cycle Assurance is a requirement that the FIPS product life cycle from design, development, manufacture through to use and disposal has been documented. This assurance includes items like configuration management for version control, in-line source code documentation, test plans, and user or admin guides. The detailed requirements for the Life Cycle Assurance documentation are covered in A.2.11 of ISO/IEC 19790:2012.

## 2.8  Finite State Model

The finite state model requirement covers both the documentation and design. The high-level operation modes must be documented in terms of a finite state machine, describing the transitions between operating modes. This also dictates the design since there are requirements and limitations concerning transitions between operating states.

Chapter 3 goes into great detail on designing and documenting compliant with the finite state machine requirements.

# CHAPTER 3

# Finite State Models

A finite state model (FSM) description of the module describes the operational and error states and how the module can transition between states.

The FIPS standard lists eight mandatory states: power on/off, general initialization, crypto officer, CSP entry, user, approved, self-test, and error.

A state like "approved" seems orthogonal to other states and so could be part of an approved/unapproved pair of states.

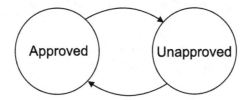

***Figure 3-1.*** *Approved/Unapproved System State FSM*

The other states would exist at the same time, with the module within the approved or unapproved state. Figure 3-2 gives an example of an FSM with a transition from power on to self-test to a quiescent state that moves to a service state when asked to and error and power off states that can be visited from any other state except the power on/power off pair of states.

© David Johnston and Richard Fant 2024

D. Johnston and R. Fant, *Designing to FIPS-140*, https://doi.org/10.1007/979-8-8688-0125-9_3

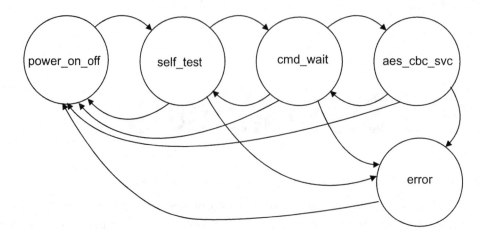

**Figure 3-2.**  *Simplified System FSM*

This shows an additional problem with requiring a single FSM for orthogonal sets of states. Some states, like the Power-Off state can be visited from any other state, creating a rat's nest of state transition arcs.

It would be clearer to use a forced transition symbol to indicate a state that is entered from any other state when a particular condition occurs.

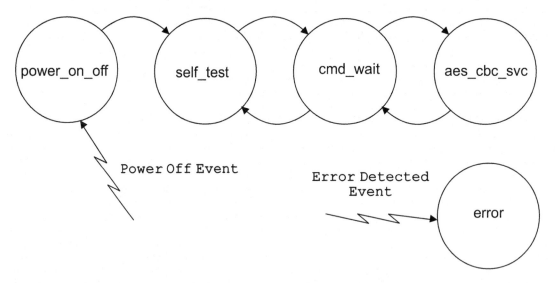

**Figure 3-3.**  *Simplified System FSM with Forced Transitions*

... *specified using a Finite State Model (or equivalent) represented by a ...*

The "or equivalent" following the term finite state model could be considered a permission to represent your system states as a superposition of multiple FSMs since it is possible to show equivalence between multiple parallel FSMs and a more complex FSM, provided the FSMs run synchronously such that they accept and respond when necessary to the same stream of events.

Using this kind of forced arc symbol makes the state transitions and general organization of the FSM look cleaner and easier to understand.

Consider the two state definitions for the user state and the approved state as defined in 7.11.4 [11.10], ISO 19790:2012EN:

> **User state:** (if a User role is implemented): a state in which authorised users obtain security services, perform cryptographic operations, or perform other approved functions.
>
> **Approved state:** a state in which approved security functions are performed.

The ISO 19790 section is not clear on this point: Would not an authorized user obtaining a security service from the module be expecting the module to be in the approved state? If the service state had to be separate from the approved state, that would not be possible. There could be service states in the approved state and service states in the unapproved state. This would double the number of service states and lead to a more complicated diagram (it does). You are free to express your state diagram in the form that you choose as long as it meets the requirements. The primary FSM requirement is in ISO IEC 19790:2012 Section 7.11.4.

> The operation of a cryptographic module **shall [11.08]** be specified using a Finite State Model (or equivalent) represented by a state transition diagram and a state transition table and state descriptions. The FSM **shall [11.09]** be sufficiently detailed to demonstrate that the cryptographic module complies with all of the requirements of this International Standard.

The requirements in the standard are many. If you had an implementation of AES in your design, trying to describe the full details of the AES algorithms in a state machine would be very difficult and inefficient. While a FIPS standard may require a particular algorithm, you should focus on the shall statements directly in the ISO/IEC 19790:2012 document with the related IGs for guidance on making a compliant system FSM and less on its referenced documents.

In addition, 7.11.4 [11.08] requires you to implement a state transition table. This gives the states and against each state the possible transitions out from the state and into the state and the conditions and events that cause each transition along with any additional text needed to show how each state and transition meets the requirements of ISO/IEC 19790:2012.

Table 3-1 shows the possible FSM transition table entries for a self-test state and an aes_256_ecb_service. A real FSM transition table would include many more transitions.

***Table 3-1.*** *FSM Transition Table Example*

| State | Description | Transition | Event |
|-------|-------------|------------|-------|
| **s_self_test** | Run a series of known-answer tests against the AES-256 block cipher | s_general_initialization → s_self_test | General initialization completes |
| | | s_self_test → s_quiescent | Successful completion of self-tests |
| | | quiescent → self_test | A service request for an on-demand test is entered into the module |
| | | self_test → error_state | A nonrecoverable failure detected by the self-tests |
| | | error_state → self test | |
| **aes_256_ecb_svc** | Module encrypts or decrypts are according to the AES256 algorithm as described in FIPS 192 | quiescent → aes_256_ecb_svc | AES256 ECB encrypt or decrypt is requested while in the quiescent state |
| | | aes_256_ecb_svc → quiescent | AES256 ECB encrypt or decrypt completes |

# 3.1  Mandatory States

The mandatory states are required in 7.11.4 [11.10].

> *The FSM of a cryptographic module **shall [11.10]** include, as a minimum, the following operational and error states.*

## 3.1.1  Power On/Off State

> ***Power on/off state:*** *A state in which the module is powered off, placed in standby mode (volatile memory maintained), or the operational state preserved in non-volatile memory (e.g., hibernation mode) and in which primary, secondary, or backup power is applied to the module. This state may distinguish between power sources being applied to a cryptographic module. For a software module, power on is the action of spawning an executable image of the cryptographic module.*

From the description given, the power on/off state does not need to correspond to the power being on or off. "Off" can include being powered but suspended. A transition from "off" to "on" can be a transition from the program not running to the program being executed. It seems safe to infer that for a level 1 software module, the mapping of on/off to being executed/not being executed is sound. However, for a hardware module where there is a clear meaning of "on" and "off," the power on/off state should be mapped to real power states of the hardware.

## 3.1.2  General Initialization State

> ***General initialization state:*** *A state in which the cryptographic module is undergo20g initializing before the module transitions to the approved state.*

What initializing means in a module depends very much on the details of the module. A pure hardware module may deem initialization to be the state visited on the clock cycle after the reset signal is deasserted. A software or hybrid module may need to request and obtain memory, initialize any devices like RNGs (random number generators) or crypto offload hardware, run software integrity tests, and so on. The one thing clear is that the module is not in an approved state until the general initialization is complete. So, the initialization should not be handling SSPs or CSPs.

The startup sequence will probably look something like

1. Power on/off

2. General initialization

3. Approved mode

4. Self-test

5. Service states

Or

1. Power on/off

2. General initialization

3. Self-test

4. Non-approved service states

# 3.1.3 Crypto Officer State

**Crypto Officer State:** *A state in which the Crypto Officer services are performed (e.g. cryptographic initialization, secure administration, and key management).*

The crypto officer state is quite self-explanatory. It is the mode in which the crypto officer does things that only crypto officers do. This is a mandatory state. Not surprisingly, there is also a FIPS requirement that a crypto officer role exists. Ironically, there is not a FIPS requirement that a user role exists.

The CMVP will usually question what tasks the crypto officer is allowed or required to execute. These tasks need to be documented in the Security Policy and/or in the Administrator Guidance for the module. These crypto officer tasks typically range from the first initialization of the module in the field to the final decommissioning or end of life of the module.

## 3.1.4 CSP Entry State

> **CSP entry state:** *A state for entering the CSPs into the cryptographic module.*

This is another mandatory state that may or may not be needed. If you have CSPs to enter (e.g., setting up a password, entering a private key, etc.), then this is the state for that. The actual entry (and output) of CSPs is in ISO/IEC 19790:2012 Section 7.9.5 (page 44).

Keep in mind that this is not called the SSP entry state. If you have a procedure for entering PSPs, you will need a state for that, but a PSP entry state is not mandatory, while the CSP entry state is.

## 3.1.5 User State

> **User state (if a User role is implemented):** *A state in which authorized users obtain security services, perform cryptographic operations, or perform other approved functions.*

This state begins with a specification language faux pas. Under a mandatory **Shall** statement (7.11.4 [11.10]) it begins with "(if a User role is implemented)." So, is it only mandatory if a user role is implemented or is the state mandatory, but has nothing to do if there is no user role defined? Clearly, if the user role is defined, the state is mandatory, but the case where the user role is not defined is not covered in the text.

## 3.1.6 Approved State

> **Approved state:** *A state in which approved security functions are performed.*

This is another state that overlaps with other states such as the user state or service states. In the approved state, only approved services and algorithms can be used.

Entry to the approved state is from the general initialization state.

> **General initialization state:** *A state in which the cryptographic module is undergoing initializing **before the module transitions to the approved state**.*

Also, reentry to the approved state can follow a maintenance operation as per Appendix B.2.7 Physical Security:

> *Specify the operator role responsible for securing and having control at all times of any unused seals and the direct control and observation of any changes to the module such as reconfigurations where the tamper evident seals or security appliances are removed or installed to ensure the security of the module is maintained during such changes and **the module is returned to a FIPS Approved state.***

## 3.1.7 Self-Test State

> **Self-test state:** *A state in which the cryptographic module is performing self-tests.*

There are user-defined self-tests and FIPS 140-3 mandated self-tests. In the self-test state, the mandatory self-tests must be run at a minimum. Any additional user-defined self-tests can be run in the self-test state, but there could also be other self-tests running continuously and self-tests running in other states like the general initialization state.

## 3.1.8 Error State

The error state is where the module goes to handle errors, but the following text makes it clear that an error state need not be terminal. The error state comes with its own shall statement [11.11] requiring that if you can recover from an error, you must.

> **Error state:** *A state when the cryptographic module has encountered an error condition (e.g., failed a self-test). There may be one or more error conditions that result in a single module error state. Error states may include "hard" errors that indicate an equipment malfunction and that may require maintenance, service, or repair of the cryptographic module or recoverable "soft" errors that may require initialization or resetting of the module. Recovery from error states **shall [11.11]** be possible, except for those caused by hard errors that require maintenance, service, or repair of the cryptographic module.*

With errors arising from self-tests applied to deterministic logic or algorithms, it may not be immediately obvious whether the error is hard or soft, so self-tests may be retried up to some limit of retries. If it stays broken, it's an error that may be hard or may be soft and needs a restart or power cycle of the module to recover.

This leads to four kinds of error handling:

1.  Soft errors that resolve immediately on retry. Don't enter the error state.

2.  Soft errors that require a restart or power cycle of the module. This may or may not need operator intervention. Do enter the error state.

3.  Hard errors that require operator intervention to repair, correct, or decommission the module. Do enter the error state.

4.  Errors have surpassed some threshold which causes the module to enter a degraded operation mode. This mode is optional but will typically have a minimum number of services available. Do enter the error state.

The context of a module will impact how errors are classified and handled. An orbiting satellite with a high rate of soft errors arising from cosmic rays would expect the self-tests to encounter soft errors. So self-tests would be applied repeatedly, and an individual soft error may not lead to an error state but might be logged for reporting. A larger number of errors may be determined to pass some threshold and lead to the module entering the error state. A computer running in a data center at ground level with environmental controls may expect no errors and mark any test failure as an error and enter the error state.

With nondeterministic functions, for example, the noise source in an RNG or the unstable bits in a PUF, the self-tests have to distinguish random variation from errors. In this example, any self-test will have some false negative and false positive error rate, so a designer should keep these error types in mind and develop an error response that gives appropriate responses.

## 3.1.9  Optional States

There are two states that are listed as optional: the bypass state and the quiescent state.

> **Bypass state:** *A state in which a service, as a result of module configuration or operator intervention, causes the plaintext output of a particular data or status item that would normally be output in encrypted form.*

While the bypass state suggests a behavior that would violate a number of "shalls" regarding the protection of SSPs and CSPs, this state is typically implemented for

1. Outputting plaintext versions of system values including CSPs and SSPs in a non-approved mode or diagnostic mode. Zeroization requirements for SSPs and CSPs when leaving the approved mode protect those values from release.

2. Collecting "raw data" from the noise source of an SP800-90B entropy source for offline analysis and/or submission for entropy certification as described in Chapters 8 and 9 of this book.

> **Quiescent state:** *A state in which the cryptographic module is dormant (e.g., low power, suspended, or in hibernation).*

The quiescent state description is using words like "suspended" and "hibernation" that come from the PC power model. If the hardware of a module is a PC running an operating system that supports power management, then these states are easily defined in terms of the existing states. It does mean that the module software will be required to interact with the operating system's power management APIs to ensure transitions into and out of a quiescent state follow the FSM described for the module.

# 3.2 Other States You Are Going to Need

For each cryptographic-related service implement in your module, you will need a corresponding state. Examples are shown in Table 3-2.

***Table 3-2.*** *Approved Service State Examples*

| Service Name | Function |
|---|---|
| hmac_sha256_svc_app | HMAC-SHA256 in approved mode |
| hmac_sha256_val_svc_app | Validate an HMAC-SHA256 signature in approved mode |
| hmac_sha512_svc_app | HMAC-SHA512 in approved mode |
| hmac_sha512_val_svc_app | Validate an HMAC-SHA512 signature in approved mode |
| hmac_sha3_512_svc_app | HMAC-SHA3/512 in approved mode |
| hmac_sha3_512_val_svc_app | Validate an HMAC-SHA3/512 signature in approved mode |
| drbg_instantiate_svc_app | Instantiate SP800-90A DRBG |
| drbg_generate_svc_app | Get random numbers from SP800-90A DRBG |
| drbg_reseed_svc_app | Request a reseed of an SP800-90A DRBG |
| ecdsa_p256_sign_svc_app | Sign data with ECDSA Curve P256 |
| ecdsa_p256_val_svc_app | Validate an ECDSA P256 signature |
| tls_open_ecdh_ccm_svc_app | Open a TLS session |
| tls_close_ecdh_ccm_svc_app | Close a TLS session |
| tls_tx_svc_app | Transmit on an open TLS session |
| tls_rx_svc_app | Receive from an open TLS session |

For non-approved services, you will also need a state. Examples are shown in Table 3-3.

**Table 3-3.** *Non-approved Service State Examples*

| Service Name | Function |
|---|---|
| sm4_ecb_enc_svc_nonapp | Encrypt with the SM4 block cipher |
| sm4_ecb_dec_svc_nonapp | Decrypt with the SM4 block cipher |
| sm3_digest_svc_nonapp | Generate a digest with the SM3 hash |
| sm3_validate_svc_nonapp | Validate an SM3 digest |

Non-approved services in a FIPS 140 context may actually be an approved service in other regulatory domains. It is common for cryptographic modules to be designed to support the algorithms of multiple regulatory domains and assign the set of approved modes differently in each regulatory domain. China, the United States, Europe, and Russia are all examples of regulatory domains with different approved algorithms. There are algorithms common to some of these domains, principally those defined through ISO WG27.

For diagnostic functions, you will need FSM states, generally in a non-approved mode of operation. For each approved algorithm, CAVP certification will be needed, and this involves providing a function to allow the injection of CAVP request vectors and recover the response vector. For, say, an AES-CBC service, there will need to be support for CAVP both over AES-CBC and over the underlying AES-ECB block cipher.

**Table 3-4.** *CAVP Vector Test State Example*

| Service Name | Function |
|---|---|
| aes_ecb_cavp_req_nonapp | Enter CAVP request vectors into the AES block cipher |
| aes_ecb_cavp_resp_nonapp | Read out the CAVP response vectors for the AES block cipher |

For RNGs, ESV certification will be needed, and this will require the collection of raw entropy data for SP800-90B IID or non-IID entropy assessment and the collection of restart data for SP800-90B restart testing, and if any non-approved conditioners are used, data will also be needed to be collected at the output of the non-approved conditioner.

**Table 3-5.** *Raw Data Collection State Example*

| Service Name | Function |
| --- | --- |
| conditioner_output_bypass_noapp | Route conditioner output to the diagnostic output in non-approved mode |
| noise_source_bypass_noapp | Route noise source output to the diagnostic output in non-approved mode |

# CHAPTER 4

# Approved Algorithms

A module implementation will include cryptographic and non-cryptographic algorithms. The non-cryptographic algorithms are typically the glue that connects the cryptographic algorithms to the module interfaces, self-test logic, zeroization logic, and data handling. Beyond the requirements for maintaining the module boundary and describing the system as a finite state model (not considering the FSM exception for Security Level 4), there is no CMVP certification requirement for the non-cryptographic algorithms.

The cryptographic algorithms that are in scope must be from the list of approved cryptographic algorithms. The specific algorithms for ISO 19790:2012 can vary depending on the regulatory domain (e.g., the country) with the different countries requiring different algorithms. For FIPS 140-3, NIST and FIPS documents from the US federal government describe the approved cryptographic algorithms.

It is allowed that non-approved cryptographic algorithms be included in the boundary, but they are not in scope for FIPS 140-3 certification and must not be available when the module is in a FIPS mode of operation.

A common reason for having a mix of approved and non-approved algorithms within a module is to meet the cryptographic requirements for multiple countries or regulatory domains. For instance, a module may include an AES block cipher for US FIPS certification and SMS4 block cipher for Chinese GM/T certification. In any instance of the module, the module would be either in an unapproved mode or one of the approved modes, but not more than one approved mode at the same time since the regulations in the regulatory domains generally allow only a mutually exclusive list of algorithms. The structure for the module containing the algorithms is likely to be similar since ISO 19790:2012 is an internationally approved standard, while the choice of algorithms is left to individual regulatory domains.

© David Johnston and Richard Fant 2024
D. Johnston and R. Fant, *Designing to FIPS-140*, https://doi.org/10.1007/979-8-8688-0125-9_4

The current set of the FIPS 140-3 approved cryptographic algorithms are documented in SP800-131Ar2 "Transitioning the Use of Cryptographic Algorithms and Key Lengths" located at `https://nvlpubs.nist.gov/nistpubs/SpecialPublications/NIST.SP.800-131Ar2.pdf`.

As the name suggests, the approved set of algorithms and key lengths can change over time, and this document is revised. Alternatively, one could review the NIST CAVP website to see which cryptographic algorithms are currently certifiable under FIPS. In general, if there are no test vectors defined for an algorithm, then that algorithm is not FIPS approved. The CAVP website is located at `https://csrc.nist.gov/projects/cryptographic-algorithm-validation-program`.

A number of the most common approved algorithms are described in this chapter. The full list changes frequently and includes a large number of algorithms, so we have focused on the more frequently implemented algorithms.

# 4.1 Block Ciphers

Block ciphers in this context refers only to symmetric key block ciphers.

There are four block cipher types covered in SP800-131Ar2: two-key TDEA, three-key TDEA, Skipjack, and AES. For future work for encryption and decryption, only AES is permitted. TDEA is deprecated through 2023 and disallowed after that. Skipjack was only defined for 80-bit security and so doesn't meet current key size requirements. In addition, Skipjack proved controversial due to its key-escrow design which permitted manufacturers and governments to add a backdoor key. Figure 4-1 shows the summary table from the SP800-131Ar2 document.

| Algorithm | Status |
|---|---|
| Two-key TDEA Encryption | Disallowed |
| Two-key TDEA Decryption | Legacy use |
| Three-key TDEA Encryption | Deprecated through 2023<br>Disallowed after 2023 |
| Three-key TDEA Decryption | Legacy use |
| SKIPJACK Encryption | Disallowed |
| SKIPJACK Decryption | Legacy use |
| AES-128 Encryption and Decryption | Acceptable |
| AES-192 Encryption and Decryption | Acceptable |
| AES-256 Encryption and Decryption | Acceptable |

***Figure 4-1.*** *SP800-131Ar2 Table 1 Block Ciphers*

The pattern here is that the end state for an encryption algorithm is "disallowed" once it has been replaced with something better – AES in this case. The final state for a decryption algorithm is "Legacy use" to allow the decryption of data previously encrypted when the algorithm was allowed.

## 4.1.1 AES

***Table 4-1.*** *FIPS 197, AES Links*

| Web Page | https://csrc.nist.gov/publications/detail/fips/197/final |
|---|---|
| Document Link | https://nvlpubs.nist.gov/nistpubs/FIPS/NIST.FIPS.197.pdf |

The AES block cipher is described in the FIPS 197 standard. AES encrypts and decrypts a block of 128 bits. The key size can be 128, 192, or 256 bits. There is no flexibility on the block size, which is always 128 bits.

A block cipher is an algorithm that maps any of an ordered set of unique values 1 to 1 with a randomly ordered set of the same values which makes it a permutation of an ordered set of values. The random mapping is different and unique with each different key. The encrypt function, with a particular key, maps in one direction. The decrypt algorithm with the same key is the same mapping in the reverse direction.

For new work, AES is the only approved block cipher, while for backward compatibility to handle data previously encrypted with TDEA, TDES is permitted.

## 4.1.2  Two-Key TDEA

*Table 4-2.* *SP800-57 Part 1 rev4, TDEA Links*

| Document Link | https://nvlpubs.nist.gov/nistpubs/SpecialPublications/ NIST.SP.800-57pt1r4.pdf |
|---|---|
| Deprecation Notice | https://csrc.nist.gov/news/2017/update-to-current-use- and-deprecation-of-tdea |

The Two-Key Triple Data Encryption Algorithm (TDEA) is the triple application of the DES, the former Data Encryption Standard, using two keys. The two 56-bit keys add up to 112 bits of key, but this variant of TDEA has been shown to be insecure and is disallowed for all uses except the decryption of existing data.

Two-Key DES was deprecated for new applications in 2017 with the notice linked in the Deprecation Notice row in Table 4-2.

## 4.1.3  TDEA/3DES

*Table 4-3.* *SP800-67 rev2, TDEA Links*

| Web Page | https://csrc.nist.gov/publications/detail/sp/800-67/ rev-2/final |
|---|---|
| Document Link | https://nvlpubs.nist.gov/nistpubs/SpecialPublications/ NIST.SP.800-67r2.pdf |
| Deprecation Notice | https://csrc.nist.gov/news/2017/update-to-current- use-and-deprecation-of-tdea |

The Triple Data Encryption Algorithm (TDEA) is the triple application of the DES, the former Data Encryption Standard, using three keys. The three 56-bit keys add up to 168 bits of key, but this offers only 112 bits of security as a result of the meet-in-the-middle attack.

Triple DES was deprecated for new applications in 2017 with the notice linked in the Deprecation Notice row in Table 4-3.

# 4.2  Block Cipher Modes of Operation

## 4.2.1  Block Cipher Privacy Modes

The approved privacy block cipher modes are specified in SP800-38A and ciphertext stealing–based modes are documented in an addendum. The ciphertext stealing variants prevent expansion of the ciphertext to a whole number of block cipher modes as is the case with the modes in the base SP800-38A document.

***Table 4-4.*** *SP800-38A Block Cipher Mode Links*

| Web Page | https://csrc.nist.gov/publications/detail/sp/800-38a/final |
|---|---|
| Document Link | https://nvlpubs.nist.gov/nistpubs/Legacy/SP/nistspecialpublication800-38a.pdf |
| Addendum | https://csrc.nist.gov/publications/detail/sp/800-38a/addendum/final |

The full list of SP800-38A confidentiality modes is shown in Table 4-5.

***Table 4-5.*** *SP800-38A Confidentiality Block Cipher Modes*

| Mode | Meaning | SP800-38A Section |
|---|---|---|
| ECB | Electronic Code Book Mode | 6.1 |
| CBC | Cipher Block Chaining Mode | 6.2 |
| CFB | Cipher Feedback Mode | 6.3 |
| OFB | Output Feedback Mode | 6.4 |
| CTR | Counter Mode | 6.5 |

Ciphertext stealing privacy modes are shown in Table 4-6.

***Table 4-6.*** *SP800-38A Ciphertext Stealing Privacy Block Cipher Modes*

| Mode | Meaning | SP800-38A Addendum Section |
|---|---|---|
| CBC-CS1 | Cipher Block Chaining – Cipher Stealing 1 | 2 |
| CBC-CS2 | Cipher Block Chaining – Cipher Stealing 2 | 3 |
| CBC-CS3 | Cipher Block Chaining – Cipher Stealing 3 | 4 |

## 4.2.2  Block Cipher Authentication Modes

The approved authentication modes are CBC-MAC, CMAC, and GMAC.

***Table 4-7.*** *Block Cipher–Based Message Authentication Modes*

| Mode | Meaning | Specifying Document |
|---|---|---|
| CBC-MAC | Cipher Block Chaining Message Authentication Code | SP800-90B |
| CMAC | Cipher-based Message Authentication Code | SP800-38B |
| GMAC | Galois Message Authentication Code | SP800-38D |

CBC-MAC is not permitted for use as a Message Authentication Code except in the context of being an SP800-90B conditioning component for entropy sources.

GMAC is not explicitly described in SP800-38D. It is described in the specification as a particular parameterization of the GCM AEAD (Authenticated Encryption with Associated Data) mode, with only plaintext data and no private data.

## 4.2.3  Block Cipher Authenticated Encryption Modes (AEAD Modes)

The approved authenticated encryption modes are CCM and GCM.

*Table 4-8.* *SP800-38A Authenticated Encryption with AEAD Block Cipher Modes*

| Mode | Meaning | Specifying Document |
|------|---------|---------------------|
| CCM | Counter with Cipher Block Chaining Message Authentication Code | SP800-38C |
| GCM | Galois Counter Mode | SP800-38D |

Both CCM and GCM provide privacy for a part of a message, while the remainder is in plaintext, along with message authentication over the whole message. This is a useful construct in packet communications, where the header of a packet is needed to be in plaintext, so that intermediate network nodes can route the packet, while the remainder of the packet (i.e., its payload) is encrypted. GCM provides a more parallelizable structure than CCM; however, the security strength of the message authentication tag is weaker than with CCM. CCM was first used as the default cipher in the WiFi 802.11i link cipher. GCM is used primarily where high throughput is needed, such as the 802.1AE MACsec link cipher. They have both long been adopted into TLS.

# 4.3  Hash Functions

NIST specifies SHA-1, SHA-2, and SHA-3. Weaknesses in SHA-1 lead to approved uses being limited. Notwithstanding the following exception for SP800-90A, all the algorithms in the SHA-2 family are approved. There is SHA-224, SHA-256, SHA-384, SHA-512, SHA-512/224, and SHA-512/256. The number indicates the size of the output. Where there are two numbers, it indicates a larger internal size with the size of the truncated output.

SHA3 includes four approved functions SHA3-224, SHA3-256, SHA3-384, and SHA3-512. In the SHA-3 specification, there are also two extendable output functions (XOF): SHAKE128 and SHAKE256. The shakes are not approved for any use except as defined by NIST, but NIST makes the following promise:

> *The XOFs can be specialized to hash functions, subject to additional security considerations. Guideline for using the XOFs will be provided in the future.*

Those approved uses were later specified as the derived functions in SP800-185 – see Section 1.6.4.

NIST's hash function web page posts its policy which was last updated in 2015 after the SHA-3 competition had concluded in Keccak being chosen for SHA-3:

https://csrc.nist.gov/Projects/Hash-Functions/NIST-Policy-on-Hash-Functions

SP800-131A Rev 2 gives a permission table in Section 9, Table 8, which is reproduced for convenience in Figure 4-2.

| Hash Function | Use | Status |
|---|---|---|
| SHA-1 | Digital signature generation | Disallowed, except where specifically allowed by NIST protocol-specific guidance. |
| | Digital signature verification | Legacy use |
| | Non-digital-signature applications | Acceptable |
| SHA-2 family (SHA-224, SHA-256, SHA-384, SHA-512, SHA-512/224 and SHA-512/256) | Acceptable for all hash function applications | |
| SHA-3 family (SHA3-224, SHA3- | Acceptable for all hash function applications | |

***Figure 4-2.***  *SP800-131A Rev 2. Table 8. Hash Functions*

The ten algorithms SHA-1, SHA-224, SHA-256, SHA-512, SHA-512/224, SHA-512/256, SHA3-224, SHA3-256, SHA3-384 and SHA3-512 are defined in the same specification FIPS 180-4.

*Table 4-9.* *FIPS 180 SHS Links*

| Web Page | https://csrc.nist.gov/publications/detail/<br>fips/180/4/final |
|---|---|
| Document Link | https://nvlpubs.nist.gov/nistpubs/FIPS/NIST.FIPS.<br>180-4.pdf |
| Hash Function Policy | https://csrc.nist.gov/Projects/Hash-Functions/<br>NIST-Policy-on-Hash-Functions |

## 4.3.1  The SHA-1 Hash Function

SHA-1 is specified in FIPS 180-4. It takes an input message with any length from 0 to $2^{64}$-1 bits and outputs a 160-bit hash digest.

SHA-1 was deprecated by NIST in 2011. SHA-1 is vulnerable to collision attacks, and practical known prefix attacks have been demonstrated. The NIST hash function policy web page indicates SHA-1 is restricted to use for interworking with legacy systems, KDFs (Key Derivation Functions), HMACs (Hash-based Message Authentication Codes), and DRBGs (Deterministic Random Bit Generators).

> *SHA-1*: *Federal agencies* ***should*** *stop using SHA-1 for generating digital signatures, generating time stamps and for other applications that require collision resistance. Federal agencies may use SHA-1 for the following applications: verifying old digital signatures and time stamps, generating and verifying hash-based message authentication codes (HMACs), key derivation functions (KDFs), and random bit/number generation. Further guidance on the use of SHA-1 is provided in SP 800-131A.*

## 4.3.2  SHA224 and SHA256 Hash Functions

SHA224 and SHA256 are essentially the same algorithm, with different initial constants and the output of SHA224 being truncated. For both algorithms, the input block size is 512, the internal state is 256 bits, and the output size is 256 bits.

## 4.3.3  SHA384, SHA512, SHA512/224, SHA512/256 Hash Functions

SHA384, SHA512, SHA512/224, and SHA512/256 are all essentially the same algorithm with different initial constants and output truncation on all except SHA512. For all four algorithms, the input block size is 1024 bits, and the internal state is 512 bits. The output size of SHA384 is 384 bits truncated from 512. The output size of SHA512/224 is 224 bits truncated from 512. The output size of SHA512 is 512 bits. The output size of SHA512/256 is 256 truncated from 512.

## 4.3.4  SHA3 Hash Function

The four SHA3 algorithms SHA3-224, SHA3-256, SHA3-384, and SHA3-512 are the most recent of the NIST approved hash algorithms and became a NIST standard in 2015 as FIPS 202.

*Table 4-10.*  *FIPS 202 SHA3 Links*

| Web Page | https://csrc.nist.gov/publications/detail/fips/202/final |
|---|---|
| Document Link | https://nvlpubs.nist.gov/nistpubs/FIPS/NIST.FIPS.202.pdf |

The output sizes of the four algorithms match that of the existing SHA algorithms and are intended to be usable as drop-in replacements. The internal state sizes of the algorithms appear to be twice that of the output size as seen in Table 4-11.

*Table 4-11.*  *SHA3 Output Sizes and Capacities*

| Algorithms | Output Size | State Size |
|---|---|---|
| SHA3-224 | 224 | 448 |
| SHA3-256 | 256 | 512 |
| SHA3-384 | 384 | 768 |
| SHA3-512 | 512 | 1024 |

# 4.3.5  SHAKE128 and SHAKE256

SHAKE128 and SHAKE256 when first published in FIPS 202 were unusual in that NIST did not specify an approved direct use for the algorithms, even though they were specified in a current FIPS standard. SP800-185 Section 1.6.4 describes derived functions. Later, two functions that use SHAKEs along with two intermediate functions were published. cSHAKES which in turn are used by TupleHash and ParallelHash were published and are described in Sections 4.3.6 through and 4.3.8. Also, recent statements from NIST to CMUF indicate that they are considering XOFs as being permitted constructs for DRBGs in SP800-90A.

Two algorithms are defined:

1.   SHAKE128($X, L$)

2.   SHAKE256($X, L$)

where $X$ is the input data and $L$ is the requested output length of the hash in bits.

NIST calls the shakes XOFs (extendable output functions). Each shake takes an input and a length to indicate how many bits to output. The output sequence for a given input string remains the same regardless of the length. The length controls how much of the output you see.

SHAKE128(input_string, 384) = A, B, C

SHAKE128(input_string, 640) = A, B, C, D, E

The values A, B, and C are the same for both invocations.

Running a command-line implementation of SHAKE128 shows this:

```
$ echo "astring" | ./shake128 16
975755bf391ca233ea47ea96b088a520
$ echo "astring" | ./shake128 32
975755bf391ca233ea47ea96b088a520dc03247469514f772e614d2d62e508dc
```

This property makes the shakes unsafe for use in some contexts. It is used as a subfunction within the algorithms described in SP800-185.

## 4.3.6 SHA3 Derived Functions

cSHAKE128 and cSHAKE256 are described in Section 3 of SP800-185. cSHAKE adds two parameters to SHAKE – N for "name" and S for "customization bitString." Varying two extra parameters leads to a different output from the SHAKE algorithms. With N and S set to empty strings, the cSHAKE algorithms return the same value as the SHAKE algorithms. Two algorithms are defined:

1. cShake128($X, L, N, S$)

2. cShake256($X, L, N, S$)

The output of cSHAKE$n(X,L,N1,S1)$ and the output of cSHAKE$n(X,L,N2,S2)$ will be unrelated, where $N1$ and $N2$ differ or $S1$ and $S2$ differ.

The FIPS 140 approved use of the two cSHAKE algorithms is strictly limited to NIST defined purposes, with values for $N$ given by NIST. Those values are given in the definitions of KMAC (Keccak-based Message Authentication Code), TupleHash, and ParallelHash. So, in practice, the two cSHAKE algorithms are unavailable for general approved use, and SP800-185 only provides three generally usable algorithms, not four, KMAC, TupleHash, and ParallelHash. These in turn use cSHAKE as an inner algorithm, and finally the cSHAKE algorithms use the SHAKE algorithms from FIPS 202. It seems like SP800-185 should have been encapsulated within FIPS 202, but maybe was released as a separate document due to the algorithms being developed later than the FIPS 202 algorithms. SP800-185 was published over a year after FIPS 202, in December 2016.

## 4.3.7 TupleHash

TupleHash is defined in SP800-185, Section 5. TupleHash takes three parameters: $X$, the tuple to be hashed; $L$ the length of the output in bits; and $S$, a customization string. Four algorithms are defined:

1. TupleHash128($X, L, S$)

2. TupleHash256($X, L, S$)

3. TupleHashXOF128($X, L, S$)

4. TupleHashXOF256($X, L, S$)

The 128-bit variants use cShake128 internally, and the 256-bit variants use cShake256. The XOF variants are the same as the non-XOF variants with the exception that the length parameter $L$ is unlimited in the XOF variant; otherwise, $L$ is limited to be less than $2^{2040}$ bits.

The TupleHash gives unrelated output for differently structured tuples. For instance, a single input "abcdef" would hash to an output unrelated to a hashed tuple "abc", "def". Similarly, "abc", "def" would hash to an output unrelated to a hashed tuple of "ab", "cdef".

While TupleHash is a defined NIST hash function, it is not listed as FIPS approved for use as a hash in other documents, for example, for the hash in SP800-90A Hash DRBG or the SP800-90B hash-based conditioner, where the specific hash functions have been restricted to particular variants of SHA2 and SHA3.

# 4.3.8 ParallelHash

ParallelHash is defined in SP800-185 Section 6. It defines a scheme for hashing large amounts of data with a parallelizable algorithm. For smaller amounts of data, ParallelHash is likely to be slower since data will be hashed twice.

Four functions are specified:

1. ParallelHash128($X,B,L,S$)

2. ParallelHash256($X,B,L,S$)

3. ParallelHashXOF128($X,B,L,S$)

4. ParallelHashXOF256($X,B,L,S$)

$X$ is the input data. $B$ is the block size into which the input data is split. $L$ is the output length, and $S$ is the customization bitstring.

The input data is split into $B$ blocks, and those blocks are independently hashed with cSHAKE and the outputs concatenated. The resulting concatenated string (which should be much shorter than the total input data for ParallelHash to offer a speed improvement) is hashed with cSHAKE to get the final output.

The XOF variants remove the internal encoding that differentiates between different lengths of output, so arbitrary amounts of output data can be computed through setting L=L1. Calling with increased L=L2 will yield the same initial L1 bits with additional L2-L1 bits appended to the output. The additional L2-L1 bits can be computed independent of the initial L1 bits, by modifying the implementation of the algorithm appropriately.

# 4.4 Limitations of Hash Use in SP800-90A

SP800-90A indicates that any approved hash function can be used in an SP800-90A Hash-DRBG or HMAC-DRBG. However, the FIPS 140-3 Implementation Guidance (IG) Annex DR (https://csrc.nist.gov/csrc/media/Projects/cryptographic-module-validation-program/documents/fips%20140-3/FIPS%20140-3%20IG.pdf) places restriction on the hash functions that can be used for SP800-90A DRBGs.

### D.R Hash Functions Acceptable for Use in the SP 800-90A DRBGs

| | |
|---|---|
| Applicable Levels: | *All* |
| Original Publishing Date: | *May 16, 2022* |
| Effective Date: | *May 16, 2022* |
| Last Modified Date: | |
| **Transition End Dates** | *May 16, 2023 – See Below* |
| Relevant Assertions: | *AS02.20, AS09.06, AS09.09* |
| Relevant Test Requirements: | *TE's associated with AS's above* |
| Relevant Vendor Requirements: | *VE's associated with AS's above* |

***Figure 4-3.*** *Implementation Guidance (IG) DR Hash Functions in SP800-90A*

---

*Since there is no efficiency gain to be had from using a truncated output within an SP800-90A DRBG, this IG limits the options for SP800-90A to only the non-truncated variants.*

---

# 4.4.1 Permitted Hashes in SP800-90A DRBGs

- For SHA-2, the only permitted options are SHA-1, SHA-256, and SHA-512.

- For SHA-3, the only permitted options are SHA3-256 and SHA3-512.

No mention is given for TupleHash or ParallelHash, so it is not clear whether or not these SHA3 derivatives are usable in SP800-90A. Given the lack of need for tuple processing and the relatively short input lengths used for hashes in SP800-90A, there is no particular need to use TupleHash or ParallelHash, but the specification is deficient in not making the requirements unambiguous.

## 4.4.2  Disallowed Hashes in SP800-90A DRBGs

This IG disallows the following hash algorithms in SP800-90A DRBGs: SHA-1, SHA-224, SHA-512/224, SHA-512/256, SHA-384, SHA3-224, and SHA3-384. In the SHA-2 case, existing certifications in process can use the truncated hashes, but all new certifications must use only the hashes permitted in the IG. What is left unsaid in this IG is anything about SP800-90B which defines conditioning components that can use the preceding hash functions. A cautious designer might choose to avoid the truncated hash algorithms in an SP800-90B conditioning component implementation to just those permitted in IG DR to avoid them being disallowed by NIST in the future.

# 4.5  Message Authentication Codes

NIST specifies five classes of symmetric MAC (Message Authentication Code):

1.  *CBC-MAC*: Cipher Block Chaining Message Authentication Code

2.  *CMAC*: Cipher-based Message Authentication Code

3.  *HMAC:* Keyed-Hash Message Authentication Code

4.  *KMAC*: Keccak-based Message Authentication Code

5.  *GMAC*: Galois Message Authentication Code

Each MAC takes a key and input data and produces a fixed size authentication code that can be verified by an entity that holds the same key. This is often used in protocols where a key agreement protocol has been used to share a secret key.

## 4.5.1  CBC-MAC Cipher Block Chaining Message Authentication Code

CBC-MAC is an exception to the other MACs in that it is not approved for general use. It is only approved for use as a vetted conditioning component in SP800-90B as part of the entropy source. In this use as a conditioner, the key need not be a secret, and there are no known plaintext issues; so, the problems with CBC-MAC when used as a MAC do not apply when it is used as a conditioner.

CBC-MAC takes and processes the input data as a sequence of blocks sized to match the block size of the cipher (128 bits in the case of AES). The first block is encrypted under the key, and the output is XORed with the next block. When used as a MAC, it is important that the IV (initialization vector) be random, but for a conditioner, this is not needed: the input data is random and is not controlled by an adversary. So, IV can be 0 and the initial stage XOR can be eliminated.

The output of the final stage encryption of the final block XORed with the previous output is the MAC.

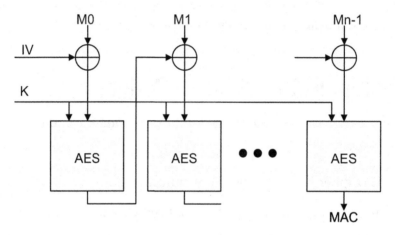

***Figure 4-4.*** *CBC-MAC Using AES*

# 4.5.2 CMAC (Cipher-Based Message Authentication Code)

***Table 4-12.*** *SP800-38B CMAC Links*

| Web Page | https://csrc.nist.gov/publications/detail/sp/800-38b/final |
|---|---|
| Document Link | https://nvlpubs.nist.gov/nistpubs/SpecialPublications/ NIST.SP.800-38B.pdf |

CMAC is specified in SP800-38B. CMAC computes a MAC using an underlying approved block cipher, which is one of the algorithms listed in SP800-38B Section 1.1. The output is no larger than the block size of the block cipher, but it may be truncated to be smaller by setting *Tlen* to be shorter than the block size of the block cipher.

One function is defined:

1.  CMAC($K$, $M$, $Tlen$)

$K$ is the key. $M$ is the message over which to compute the MAC. $Tlen$ is the requested output length of the MAC in bits.

The two new keys K1 and K2 are generated from the key $K$ and input data length. When the input data length is a multiple of the block, K1 is XORed with the final block before encryption. When the final block is padded, K2 is XORed with the final block before encryption.

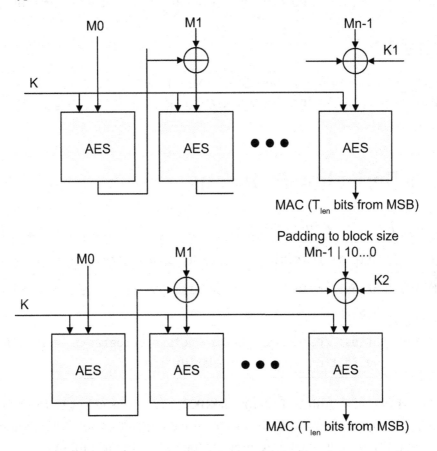

**Figure 4-5.** *CMAC Using AES, with and Without Padding*

## 4.5.3 HMAC Keyed-Hash Message Authentication Code

***Table 4-13.*** *FIPS 198-1 HMAC Links*

| Web Page | https://csrc.nist.gov/publications/detail/fips/198/1/final |
|---|---|
| Document Link | https://nvlpubs.nist.gov/nistpubs/FIPS/NIST.FIPS.198-1.pdf |

HMAC uses an underlying hash algorithm to make a MAC. The hash algorithm can be any one of the approved NIST hash functions from the SHA2 and SHA3 series of hashes.

## 4.5.4 KMAC

The KECCAK Message Authentication Code (KMAC) uses a variable length keyed-hash function and is described in SP800-185. It is based on KECCAK which is the core of the SHA3 algorithm.

# 4.6 Key Derivation Functions

***Table 4-14.*** *SP800-108 KDF Links*

| Web Page | https://csrc.nist.gov/publications/detail/sp/800-108/final |
|---|---|
| Document Link | https://nvlpubs.nist.gov/nistpubs/Legacy/SP/nistspecialpublication800-108.pdf |
| CAVP Link | https://csrc.nist.gov/projects/cryptographic-algorithm-validation-program/key-derivation |

NIST refers to KDFs within SP800-108 as KBKDFs (Key-Based Key Derivation Functions), although the term KBKDF does not appear in SP800-108. KBKDF does appear in the CAVP testing text, for example, at the CAVP URL in Table 4-14.

SP800-108 defines three KDFs (Key Derivation Functions):

1.  KDF in Counter Mode. SP800-108, Section 5.1

2.  KDF in Feedback Mode. SP800-108, Section 5.2

3.  KDF in Double-Pipeline Iteration Mode. SP800-108, Section 5.3

The KDFs are built using PRFs (pseudorandom functions). The permitted PRF algorithms are listed in SP800-108, Section 4, which states that an approved PRF may either be HMAC as defined in FIPS 198-1 or CMAC as defined in SP800-38B.

The output size of the PRF will be a fixed number of bits: for example, 80, 128, 192, 256, 384, or 512. CMAC will always have an output block size of 128 bits when used with AES. HMAC has multiple underlying hash algorithm options and output size options. The reference page in SP800-108 includes SP800-90A; however, it is not actually used anywhere in SP800-108. It seems that SP800-90A DRBGs are not approved for use as PRFs in SP800-108.

# 4.6.1  KDF in Counter Mode

The counter mode KDF invokes the underlying PRF (HMAC or CMAC) with an input bitstring that includes a substring of bits that increment with each invocation.

Enough iterations are run to gather enough bits to fulfill the requested output length L. The first (leftmost) L bits are used, and the remainder, if any, are discarded. The input bitstring is formed from [ i || label || 0x00 || context || L ] where i is the counter, starting at 1, label and context are input bitstrings used to differentiate the key derivation from any other, 0x00 is 8 zero bits, and L is the requested output length in bits.

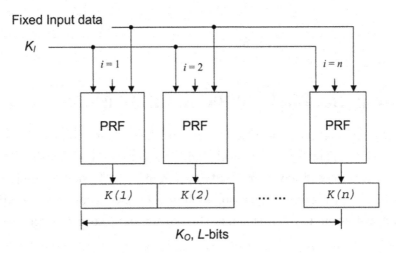

***Figure 4-6.***  *KDF in Counter Mode*

## 4.6.2  KDF in Feedback Mode

KDF in feedback mode has a similar structure to CBC mode, where the output of one stage forms part of the input to the next state. It might better be named feed forward mode or chained mode, but it is not.

The input bitstring for each PRF stage is formed from [ K(i-1) || i || Label || 0x00 || Context || L ] where K(i-1) is the previous PRF output; i is the counter, starting at 1; label and context are input bitstrings used to differentiate the key derivation from any other; 0x00 is 8 zero bits; and L is the requested output length in bits.

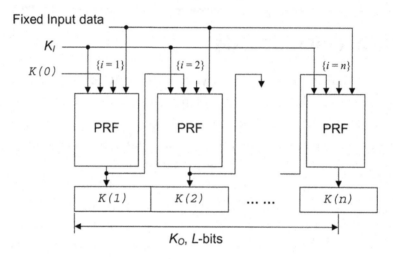

*Figure 4-7.*  *PRF in Feedback Mode*

## 4.6.3  KDF in Double Pipeline Iteration Mode

The Double Pipeline Iteration Mode KDF combines two distinct stages. The first stage takes the key and the fixed input data and chains a series of PRFs, passing the output of one PRF to the next to produce a stream of random blocks. Those random blocks form part of the input to the second stage along with the key, a counter, and the same fixed input data that was input to the first stage. The output of the second stage is the output of the algorithm.

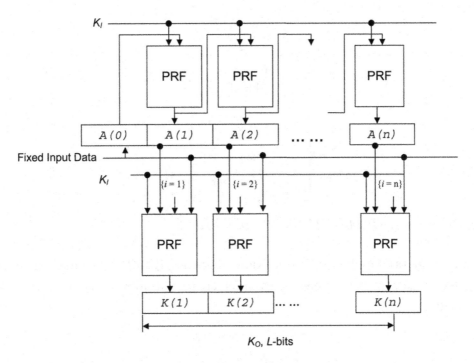

**Figure 4-8.** *PRF in Double Pipeline Iteration Mode*

## 4.6.4 Password-Based Key Derivation

**Table 4-15.** *SP800-132 PBKDF Links*

| Web Page | `https://csrc.nist.gov/publications/detail/sp/800-132/final` |
|---|---|
| Document Link | `https://nvlpubs.nist.gov/nistpubs/Legacy/SP/` `nistspecialpublication800-132.pdf` |

SP800-132 defines a KDF to derive a master key (MK) from a password or passphrase. It further specifies four approved uses, labeled options 1a, 1b, 2a, and 2b.

Option 1a uses the derived key MK directly to protect data with an approved encryption or AEAD mode.

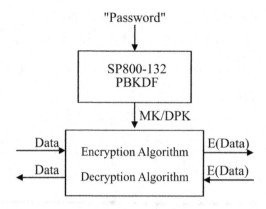

**Figure 4-9.** *Use of SP800-132 PBKDF Option 1a*

Option 1b uses a Key-Based Key Derivation Function (KBKDF) to derive one or more data protection keys from the master key, which are then used with an approved mode to protect data.

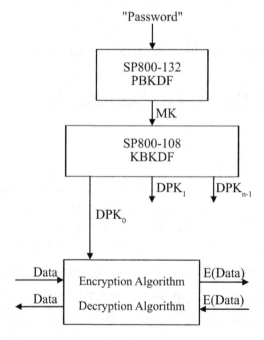

**Figure 4-10.** *Use of SP800-132 PBKDF Option 1b*

Option 2a uses the master key to decrypt an encrypted data protection key which is then used with an approved mode to protect data.

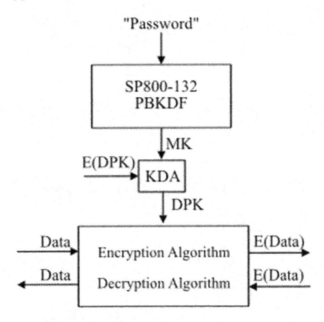

***Figure 4-11.*** *Use of SP800-132 PBKDF Option 2a*

Option 2b throws another step into the mix and uses an SP800-108 KBKDF to derive one or more keys (labeled in the diagram as KPK – key protection key), which are used to decrypt an encrypted DPK which in turn is used to protect data.

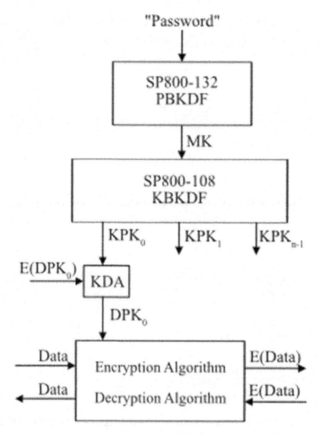

***Figure 4-12.*** *Use of SP800-132 PBKDF Option 2b*

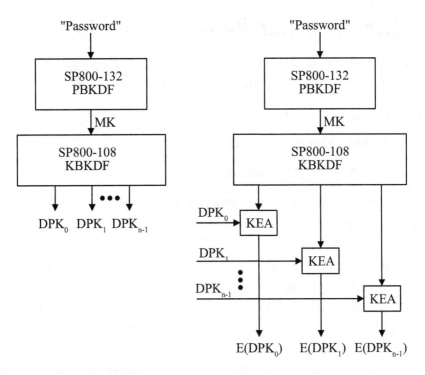

***Figure 4-13.*** *Uses of SP800-132 PBKDF*

## 4.6.5  FIPS 198-1 Hash-Based Key Derivation Function

***Table 4-16.*** *FIPS 198-1 Hash-Based Key Derivation Function Links*

| Web Page | https://csrc.nist.gov/pubs/sp/800/56/c/r2/final |
| --- | --- |
| Document Link | https://nvlpubs.nist.gov/nistpubs/SpecialPublications/ NIST.SP.800-56Cr2.pdf |

The HKDF (Hash-Based Key Derivation Function) is based on an extract-then-expand structure. It is widely used both as an Internet Engineering Task Force (IETF)-defined algorithm and a FIPS 140 approved NIST algorithm.

# 4.7  Deterministic Random Bit Generators

DRBGs (Deterministic Random Bit Generators) are specified in SP800-90A. This specifies three classes of DRBG based on different underlying functions:

1. *CTR-DRBG*: A block cipher–based DRBG

2. *HASH-DRBG*: A hash-based DRBG

3. *HMAC-DRNG*: An HMAC-based DRBG

Previously, in SP800-90A (prior to SP800-90Ar1), a fourth DRBG, the Dual-EC-DRBG, was included. This was withdrawn after it was revealed to contain a cryptographic backdoor.

The remaining DRBGs, while apparently secure, contain a lot of implementation flexibility and features that appear to make side channel and fault injection analysis more feasible. Care must be applied in the choice of parameters in the DRBG algorithms to avoid these pitfalls.

The HASH, HMAC, and CTR-DRBGs algorithms each allow up to $2^{48}$ generate requests per seed each of up to $2^{19}$ (524,288) bits. In the case of the CTR-DRBG, a $2^{19}$-bit request would lead to 4096 iterations of AES with the same key in counter mode. 4096 DPA (Differential Power Analysis) would be sufficient to mount a successful key recovery attack against some implementations. Permitting the full parameter range allowed in the SP800-90A specification for a request can lead to possible attack methods that mostly postdate the specification.

The basic outline for a PRNG is a *next_state*() function followed by an output() function. The PRNG contains a state, and the *next_state*() and *output*() functions both operate on that state. Initialization of the PRNG sets the initial state. Reseeding the PRNG updates the state with fresh entropic data. NIST SP800-90A provided different names to the usual terminology. PRNG is called DRBG while the output function is the generate function. The next state function is the update function. The initialize and reseed functions retain their names.

# CHAPTER 5

# Counter Security Features of NIST-Approved Cryptographic Algorithms

There are several requirements in FIPS 140-3 and the subordinate algorithm documents that enforce the use of vulnerable constructs or permit combinations and parameterizations that would undermine security.

The best course of action is to be aware of these issues and work around them by providing mitigations to the vulnerability and not making poor parameter and configuration choices.

## 5.1 General Principles of Poor Cryptographic Design

This chapter provides some known examples of danger points in the approved algorithms and their construction under FIPS 140-3 and suggests suitable workaround or alternatives.

### 5.1.1 Overly Flexible Compliant Implementation Choices

Some of the standards defining approved algorithms within a FIPS 140 context provide a wide amount of flexibility in algorithm design. For example, the CTR-DRBG in SP800-90A or the Entropy Conditioning Algorithms in SP800-90B effectively allow implementers enough flexibility to implement insecure designs that are still FIPS

© David Johnston and Richard Fant 2024
D. Johnston and R. Fant, *Designing to FIPS-140*, https://doi.org/10.1007/979-8-8688-0125-9_5

compliant. Always remember adhering to the FIPS 140 standards is not a guarantee that a FIPS design is secure; the designer still has to apply common sense and good security strategies.

## 5.1.2 Excessively Repetitive Use of Security-Critical Data

Modern attack techniques including side-channel methods, fault injection methods, and hybrid fault injection + side-channel methods have become the dominant effective means of attacking otherwise algorithmically secure algorithms. Any secure algorithm design should take these modern physical attacks into account and take steps to minimize key and data reuse and minimize opportunities for finding synchronization information in emissions and incorporating fault injection mitigations.

Designing such mitigations into a security system can necessitate running afoul of mandated behavior and thus certifiability. In these instances, the certification requirement will always win over design security when certifiability is a requirement.

We can look at AES-KEY-WRAP as an example of an algorithm that incorporates a built-in integrity check that affords some resistance to fault injection. Whereas the burst mode, and the start-stop nature of algorithms like AES, HMAC, and SHA-n render them prime targets for side-channel attacks when keys are reused more than necessary.

## 5.1.3 Focusing on Algorithm Transition over Data Encoding Transition

It can be seen in the lists of allowed algorithm that these old, insecure algorithms, while being disallowed or deprecated for new modules, remain permitted for backward compatibility with data encrypted or signed or authenticated using the old algorithms. This leaves insecure algorithms in circulation and renders systems vulnerable to downgrade attacks. Parallels with this have been seen in the HTTPS protocols in web browsers continuing to support the insecure RC4 algorithm in the name of interoperability.

A more security-conscious approach would be to focus on the data that had been secured with the old algorithms rather than the certification of the algorithms themselves. In addition, rules could be imposed that require the data to be re-encoded using the newer algorithms or risk losing credibility when claiming the data is more secure. For example, FIPS modules produced today will typically still support DES, 2DES, 3DES, SHA-1, and the Dual-EC-DRBG for interoperability with old data encoded using those algorithms.

## 5.1.4 Unjustified Use of Overcomplicated Cryptographic Algorithms

The choices of elliptic curves used in the NIST ECDH (Elliptic Curve Diffie Hellman) and ECDSA curves are defined with large constants for which the derivation or rationale have never been supplied. For this reason, the NIST curves are widely untrusted and not commonly used where certification compliance matters.

This suspicion is not unwarranted. The Dual-EC-DRBG was shown to be capable of harboring a backdoor through selection of a hard-to-factor composite number for one of the constants. It was later shown to be insecure in other ways with the existence of the backdoor later confirmed with leaks from the NSA.

There are now alternatives for the elliptic curves in the form of Ed25519 and X25519 for signing and key agreement which uses NUMS (Nothing Up My Sleeves) values for constants and complies with all the "safe curves" principles. In a 2019 attack called Minerva, a number of devices using NIST curves such as P256 were broken, while newer algorithms using safe curves, like X25519 and ED25519, were not.

For the Dual-EC-DRBG, other SP800-90A algorithms were available when distrust in the Dual-EC-DRBG along with its slow execution speed led to poor adoption by designers except where the NSA paid for its inclusion. If you are an implementer and an intelligence agency is offering you money to adopt a strange and untrustworthy algorithm, you might want to consider your options carefully.

## 5.1.5 KDF Double Pipeline Iteration Mode

The double pipeline iteration construct invokes twice as many PRFs for the same amount of output. This will make a design more vulnerable to side-channel attacks because the key is processed twice as many times as it would with the other two KDFs in the same document. The alternatives include the KDF in Counter Mode the KDF in Feedback Mode and HKDF.

## 5.1.6  SP800-90A Block Cipher DF

The Block Cipher DF (derivation function) repeatedly invokes CBC-MAC over the same partially entropic input data, with an index counter field added along with several other static, known values.

Adversaries who use side-channel and fault injection attacks find this helpful because it makes repetitive use of the same security critical data and key values while providing known plaintext for easy validation of key and data guesses by the attacker. This is a best-case scenario for most attackers.

In contrast, the HMAC, CBC-MAC, or CMAC conditioners described in SP800-90B, which can be used in place of the Block Cipher DF, do not suffer from unnecessary reuse of keys, process each block of input entropic data only once, and do not introduce known plaintext into the data. Improvements in conditioner algorithms might include adding integrity data to mitigate fault injection attacks, randomization of data subsets used to mitigate synchronization of side-channel data, and most importantly updating the key on each invocation of AES, so each key is used only once and multiple side-channel traces of the same key schedule cannot then be used to infer the key.

## 5.1.7  SP800-90A HMAC and HASH DRBGs

Both the HMAC and HASH DRBGs described in SP800-90A appear unnecessarily complicated, and this complication has never been justified nor explained. The primary alternative is the CTR-DRBG, but only with good parameter and configuration choices such as not permitting more than 64 outputs per generate. Future improvements in DRBG design might include the use of HKDF, which provides for a very simple algorithm description that includes key update on every output such as

$$(output, new\_K, new\_V) = HKDF(K, V, len(output)+len(K)+len(V))$$

Another possible inclusion in SP800-90A is the CHA-CHA algorithm which provides a simple CTR-HASH structure or the XOF modes of SHA-3.

## 5.1.8  CTR-DRBG

One implementation of the CTR-DRBG has been successfully violated using side-channel attacks against its key. This is because the CTR-DRBG algorithm permits the generate() request to specify how much data should be returned. The problem is that a single generate call with a large size output will run the CTR algorithm over many blocks, using the same key. This allows the adversary to request a large amount of data to cause the key to be reused many times.

The solution is to not permit the user to request large amounts of data. Only permit one block of data per generate() request. In the Intel CPU RNG that uses the CTR-DRNG, only one 128-bit block is generated between each update, so the key reuse is minimized to four invocations: one for the output data, two for the key update, and one for the V update. As a result, the Intel DRBG has so far never been successfully attacked using side-channel methodologies.

## 5.1.9 AES

There are many implementation pitfalls with AES. The S-Boxes used in cryptography have often been implemented with table lookups, which have been shown to be vulnerable with side-channel attacks. There are implementations using table lookups for other stages of the algorithm and for combining multiple stages into a single table lookup. This makes it easier to attack through side channels since the location of access provides information on the plaintext data.

The Mix Column function in AES invokes multiplication within an 8-bit Galois field with generator polynomial of 0x11b. The normal multiplication algorithm uses shifts and adds, but when a 1 is shifted off the end of the byte, 0x1b (the lower 8 bits of the generator polynomial) are XORed with the result. When implemented with a conditional if-then-else structure, this can lead to a nonconstant time stage in the algorithm that might permit side-channel timing attacks.

An alternative implementation for the S-Box is using constant time combinatorial functions for the S-Boxes, such as those by Canwright or the Logic Minimization group. These render the algorithm constant time. An alternative for the Mix Column is a constant time combinatorial function or careful constant time coding of the conditional feedback. The multiply operations in Mix Column do not need to be done with GF log tables or any other general multiplication scheme, since the multiples are only by 2 and 3. Multiply by 2 is a shift, and multiply by 3 is a shift and an XOR (since $3 = 2 + 1$).

# CHAPTER 6

# CAVP Lab

As described in Chapter 1, if a vendor wants to sell their product containing crypto algorithms to the US government, that product (or more specifically, the module containing the crypto algorithms) must be FIPS certified. For a module to be FIPS certified means that the module must also contain at least one (1) FIPS-approved crypto algorithm. And finally, all FIPS-approved crypto algorithm within the module's boundary must be validated and issued an official certificate by the CMVP. The program that provides this service is called the *Cryptographic Algorithm Validation Program* (CAVP).

The purpose of the CAVP is to validate that the FIPS-approved crypto algorithms in your module have been correctly implemented. For example, SHA-256 is a FIPS-approved crypto algorithm and is a well-known and publicly available secure hash function. However, SHA-256 could be implemented by vendors in various ways using different programming techniques or languages such as C++ or Verilog. This is where the CAVP comes in: their job is to validate that the crypto algorithm, regardless of its implementation, correctly follows the steps as outlined on the CAVP FIPS-approved algorithm website. For more details about these approved algorithms, please see Chapter 4. The current list of FIPS-approved algorithms is located at `https://csrc.nist.gov/projects/cryptographic-algorithm-validation-program`.

## 6.1 CAVP Tool Overview

The basic idea behind validating any FIPS-approved crypto algorithm is that the CAVP will generate a set of random input values which are fed into the implementation under test (IUT) as input parameters. Once the IUT has finished executing on those parameters, the output from its crypto algorithm is compared by the CAVP against a set of expected answers. If the answer matches what was expected, then the algorithm was correctly implemented. This process is called a known-answer test (KAT). Over the years, the CAVP has used different tools to accomplish this known-answer testing.

© David Johnston and Richard Fant 2024
D. Johnston and R. Fant, *Designing to FIPS-140*, https://doi.org/10.1007/979-8-8688-0125-9_6

# 6.1.1 CAVS Tool

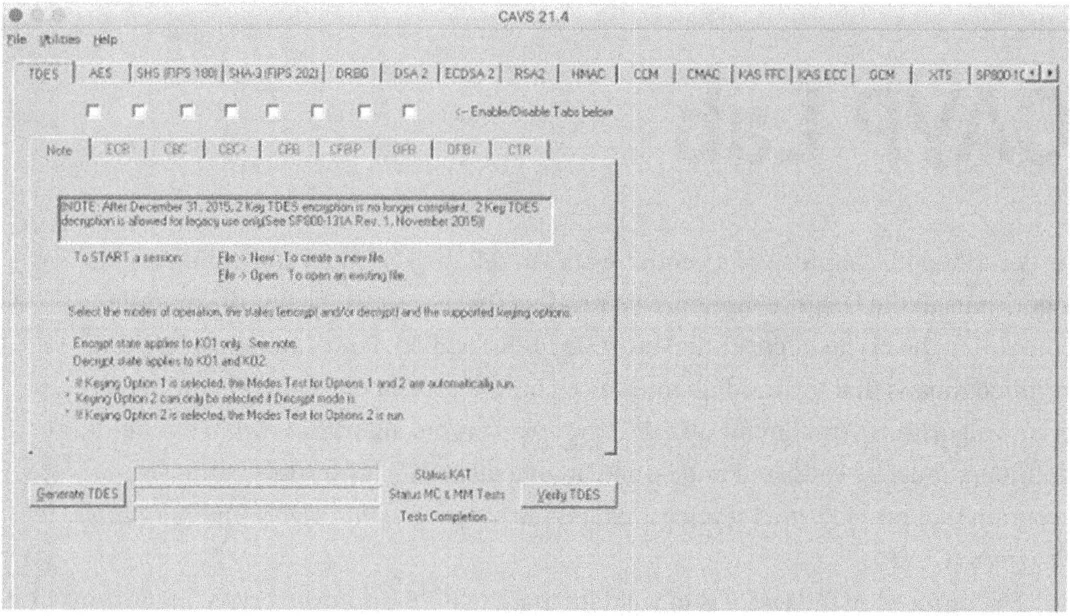

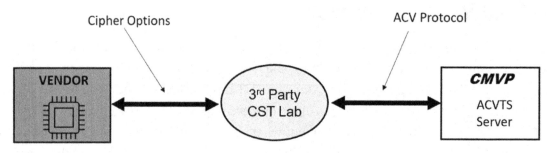

**Figure 6-1.** *CAVS Tool GUI*

The first tool developed by the CAVP for crypto algorithm validation was the
*Cryptographic Algorithm Validation System* (CAVS). Figure 6-1 shows a screenshot of
this Windows-based tool. The CAVS tool was used by Third-Party Cryptographic Security
Testing (CST) Labs to generate random test vectors and validate the answers given by
the IUT in response. The CAVS tool was retired on June 30, 2020, and a new tool took its
place: the *Automated Cryptographic Validation Test System* (ACVTS).

# 6.1.2 Automated Cryptographic Validation Test System

**Figure 6-2.** *ACVTS*

The Automated Cryptographic Validation Test System (ACVTS) has a different process flow from the CAVS tool. As depicted in the block diagram in Figure 6-2, the ACVTS consists of three main components: the vendor, the CST Lab, and the ACVTS Server. The Cipher Option interface between the Third-Party CST Lab and the vendor will vary depending on the CST Lab. The communication between the Third-Party CST Lab and the ACVTS Server is defined by the *Automated Cryptographic Validation Protocol* (ACVP). Please note that the ACVP and the CAVP are not the same thing. The ACVP is a communication protocol, while the CAVP is a program; the terms are not interchangeable.

The actual process for validating the algorithms is depicted in Figure 6-3. For the purpose of illustration, let's assume the vendor has implemented an AES Crypto Engine with three modes (ECB, CBC, CTR) and two key sizes (128, 256) in their module and wish to have it validated. Here are the high-level steps describing this process which match the step numbers in Figure 6-3.

***Figure 6-3.*** *ACVTS Process Flow*

1)  The vendor sends a request to the CST Lab specifying the algorithm and its cipher options – in this example, AES with ECB, CBC, CTR, and key sizes 128 and 256.

2)  The CST Lab passes the vendor request to the ACVTS Server using the ACVP Protocol. The ACVTS Server now generates a set of random test vectors (i.e., input parameters) based on the algorithm and cipher options specified by the vendor. In our AES example, we have six permutations: three modes and two key sizes.

3)  The ACVTS Server then passes these test vectors to the Third-Party CST Lab.

4) The CST Lab passes the test vectors on to the vendor. The test harness now parses the vectors extracting the relevant data that is used as input to the AES Crypto Engine. The AES Crypto Engine executes on these input values and eventually outputs a response. This response is formatted by the test harness to meet the ACVP standard. [The test harness and its JSON formatting are described as follows.]

5) The vendor sends the formatted response back to the CST Lab.

6) The CST Lab then passes the formatted response on to the ACVTS Server. Since this is a known-answer test, the ACVTS Server now compares the newly arrived response to the answer that is expected.

7) If the vendor response matches the server's expected answer, then a CAVP certificate is issued and passed back to the Third-Party CST Lab.

8) The CST Lab finally passes the CAVP certificate to the vendor. This is a public-facing certificate containing the vendor's name and all the details of this particular algorithm.

If the vendor's response received by the ACVTS Server does not match the expected answer, then the ACVTS will send a "fail" message back to the Third-Party CST Lab, which then passes it on to the vendor. It is not uncommon for a crypto algorithm to be implemented correctly (i.e., produce the correct answer), but have its response incorrectly formatted which generates a failure verdict. The ACVTS Server can return the following types of verdicts to the vendor for a response file, as shown in Table 6-1.

**Table 6-1.** *Verdicts Returned*

| Verdict | Meaning |
|---|---|
| Passed | All test cases in the response file have given the expected answer |
| Fail | At least one test case has failed |
| Expired | At least one test case was not received by the ACVTS before it exceeded its expiration date (usually 30 days from issue) |
| Unreceived | The server has not received responses for all the test cases |
| Incomplete | Not all test cases have been processed by the ACVTS Server |
| Error | An error occurred somewhere while processing the test session |

While Figure 6-3 shows a single ACVTS Server, there are in fact two different ACVTS Servers: one Demo Server and one Production Server. The strategy used by the ACVTS is that the vendor should only request/use test vectors from the Production Server once they have proven they can correctly request/use test vectors from the Demo Server. This is an important strategy since the CMVP doesn't want vendors to waste server bandwidth by using the Production Server to debug their crypto algorithms. Plus, there is a nontrivial chance that a vendor incorrectly using the Production Server could inadvertently cause a denial-of-service situation for other users.

In general, assuming a crypto algorithm is correctly implemented, at least three different types of test vectors will be needed to validate it:

- *1 Set of Demo Vectors with Expected Answer*: The ACVTS Demo Server issues a random set of input test vectors along with their expected output. This allows a vendor to self-verify if their crypto algorithm is implemented correctly. Because this is a self-verification, no response is expected from the vendor to the ACVTS Demo Server. This is the primary scenario used by the vendor to debug the crypto algorithm itself.

- *1 Set of Demo Vectors Without Expected Answer*: The ACVTS Demo Server issues a random set of input test vectors without the expected answer. This allows a vendor to verify if their response to the ACVTS Demo Server is correctly formatted using the ACVP protocol. It is possible to have the correct answer, but still fail if the expected ACVP format is incorrect. This scenario does require a response from the vendor to the ACVTS Demo Server within 30 days of the test vectors being issued. Once expired, the vendor will need to request a new set of test vectors.

- *1 Set of Production Vectors Without Expected Answer*: This is the final stage for validation. Once the test vectors are issued by ACVTS Production Server, the vendor has 30 days to provide a response before the test vectors expire. Once expired, the vendor will need to request a new set of test vectors. Once a verdict of pass is returned, then a certificate will be issued. But this process is not currently fully automated. A human CAVP reviewer must provide the final approval before an algorithm certificate is published. Most likely, this is done to verify the language used in the implementation definition, description, or operating environment is appropriate for a public-facing US government web page.

Please note that it is possible to receive a single CAVP certificate for all the crypto algorithms within a single module by using a single request file. Alternatively, it is also possible to receive a single CAVP certificate for each individual crypto algorithm in a module by using one request file for each crypto algorithm. This decision of which method to employ is a strategic/marketing decision that will vary by vendor.

## 6.2 First-Party CAVP Lab

The CMVP has a persistent problem: there are more FIPS modules being submitted by vendors than there are CMVP reviewers readily available to evaluate them, which *"strains the ability for a finite number of validators to provide timely turnaround."*[1] It is

---

[1] www.nccoe.nist.gov/sites/default/files/library/project-descriptions/cmvp-project-description-final.pdf

not unusual for a vendor to submit a module to the CMVP for FIPS validation and have it wait in a Review Pending queue for nine months or longer. This is obviously a huge impact on any product's road map and time to market.

One of the solutions to address this problem being implemented by the CMVP is automating as much of the validation process as possible: in other words, remove human interaction from the noncritical steps wherever possible. Some examples of where the CMVP is automating include tools such as

- *Web CRYPTIK*: Generating reports and evidence tracking for CST Labs

- Automated Entropy Source Validation Service (ESV) [see Section 8.12 of this book]

- Automated Cryptographic Validation Test System for Third-Party CST Labs (ACVTS)

The First-Party CAVP Lab validation program discussed in the next section is another step toward the CMVP automation effort.

## 6.2.1  First-Party Lab vs. Third-Party Lab

The validation process flow for a First-Party Lab is basically the same as the Third-Party Lab described in Section 1.1.2 with one significant difference: as can be seen in Figure 6-4, the Third-Party CST Lab is replaced by a First-Party CAVP Lab. The First-Party CAVP Lab is owned by the vendor who designed the module.

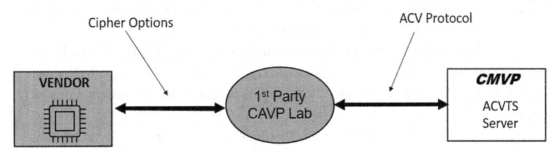

***Figure 6-4.***  *First-Party CAVP Lab*

A summary of differences between First-Party and Third-Party Labs is shown in Table 6-2. This information is current as of September 2022 and is based on input from the CMVP as well as feedback from various labs and vendors.

**Table 6-2.**  *First-Party vs. Third-Party Labs*

| Compare | Third-Party CST Lab | First-Party CAVP Lab |
|---|---|---|
| Lab Type | Commercial. Can work with any vendor | Noncommercial. Can only work with internal customers |
| Cipher Options (modes, key sizes, etc.) | If a vendor is using multiple labs, then they will need to learn multiple cipher option formats | Only one cipher option format since the vendor owns their own First-Party Lab |
| $ Cost of Test Vectors | Typically costs between $5K and $10K per product. Your mileage may vary | $10K annual flat fee for unlimited test vectors **OR** $2K for 500 test vectors |
| Time Savings | A Third-Party Lab will usually take longer since having human intermediaries adds time | With no intermediary, process will generally be faster: hours instead of days. Days instead of weeks |
| CVP Tester Accreditation | Need two CVP certified testers. This is only applicable if you are a CST Lab | Currently, there are no requirements for CVP certification of testers |

# Lab Type

A First-Party CAVP Lab is listed in the National Volunteer Lab Accreditation Program (NVLAP)[2] as a lab that is *"Not available for commercial testing."* By contrast, a Third-Party CST Lab is listed as a lab that provides a *"Commercial Testing Service."*

This is the significant difference between First-Party and Third-Party Labs: a First-Party Lab owned by a vendor can only validate crypto algorithms implemented by that vendor, while a Third-Party Lab can validate the crypto algorithm implementations of any vendor.

Please note the CAVP *algorithm* validation done by a First-Party Lab is not the same as the CMVP *module* validation done by a Third-Party CST Lab. Vendors wishing to claim FIPS certification for their modules must still use a Third-Party CST Lab to submit on their behalf to the CMVP.

---

[2] www-s.nist.gov/niws/index.cfm?event=directory.results

## Cipher Options

As an example of a cipher option, consider our earlier example of our AES Crypto Engine, where we specified three different modes (ECB, CBC, CTR) and two different key sizes (128 and 256) for a total of six permutations. While this is a trivial example of cipher options, it is easy to see how a module could easily have 100s of permutation specified. How does the vendor communicate these cipher options to their CAVP testing lab? Since there are no official guidelines for specifying those options, each Third-Party CST Lab has defined their own cipher option templates. These templates currently range from MS Word or Excel documents to web-based GUIs.

Since at present there are 18 Third-Party Labs, if a vendor is using multiple labs, then they would need to learn multiple cipher option formats. By contrast, for a First-Party Lab, only one format would be needed since the vendor can define it themselves.

## Cost of Test Vectors

This is a rough estimate of the monetary cost for all the test vectors needed for CAVP certification of a module. We know from Section 1.1.2 that at a minimum every module will require at least three sets of test vectors assuming the crypto algorithm is healthy. The costs provided in Table 6-2 are based on empirical data provided by various labs and vendors. Your costs may vary since the estimates greatly depend on the number of algorithms/permutations and the relationship/contract between the lab and the vendor.

But as a general statement and everything else being equal, if a vendor is only submitting one or two modules a year, then the recommended strategy would be to use an existing Third-Party CST Lab. On the other hand, if a vendor is submitting three or more modules a year, then a First-Party CAVP Lab might make more economic sense.

## Time Savings

This is a rough characterization, which can vary by lab, of the turnaround time: that is, ignoring the IUT execution time, how long it takes from the vendor requesting the test vectors to a vendor receiving the final verdict from the ACVTS server. There is feedback from some vendors who use Third-Party CST Labs that the turnaround time is between two and four weeks, while other vendors claimed it only took a few days. Obviously, the turnaround time greatly depends on how busy the ACVTS Server and reviewers are as well as how responsive individual Third-Party CST Labs are to their customers. By contrast, there has been feedback that using a First-Party Lab only took a few hours of turnaround time.

Since a Third-Party CST Lab mostly just serves as a pass-through for all the traffic between the vendor and the ACVTS Server, there may be limited value in using them as opposed to a First-Party Lab; in fact, using the Third-Party Lab may add considerable time to the process depending on how busy they are.

Clearly, your turnaround time may vary depending on your lab type. But as a general observation, removing a step from any process that requires human intermediaries on the whole makes the process run faster.

## CVP Tester Accreditation

The CMVP requires that every Third-Party CST Lab have Certified Validation Program (CVP) Accreditation for at least two of their testers (i.e., lab employees). These testers must pass a certification exam which covers all aspects of module validation including CAVP certification. This formal accreditation is usually transparent to most vendors.

By contrast, there are currently no CMVP requirements for CVP accreditation of testers for First-Party CAVP Labs. But this will most likely change in 2024 after a new CVP Exam is created which only tests CAVP certification knowledge instead of module validation knowledge.

# 6.2.2  Setting Up a First-Party CAVP Lab

The program specifying the requirements for setting up a First-Party CAVP Labs is known officially as **17ACVT**. This official name will appear in most of the ACVP documentation and, for the purposes of this book, can be used interchangeably with First-Party CAVP Lab.

In general, setting up a First-Party CAVP Lab (or 17ACVT Lab) is fairly straightforward. But there are few caveats to consider before continuing with this section:

- The following information is correct as of February 2022. However, FIPS is a constantly changing landscape, so some of this information may be stale by the time of publication of this book.

- Currently, there is very little 17ACVT-specific documentation available. Instead, the NVLAP is assuming anyone setting up a First-Party Lab will instead use existing Third-Party CST Lab documentation and checklists during the setup process. The idea is that the vendor should discriminate which requirements are applicable to First-Party Labs and which are not. For example, any requirements related to "*module validation*" can be safely ignored if you are just setting up a First-Party CAVP lab. Eventually, the NVLAP will have documentation and accreditation testing specific to First-Party Labs only.

```
https://csrc.nist.gov/projects/cryptographic-algorithm-validation-
program/how-to-access-acvts
```

The process for gaining access to the ACVTS production environment **as a 17ACVT laboratory** is as follows:

1. Set up a system that can fetch demo test vectors from the ACVTS Demo Server.

2. Complete the NVLAP application and submit the fees to NVLAP. Information about the 17ACVT scope can be found in Annex G of NVLAP Handbook 150-17. The application can be found on the NVLAP page. The full accreditation must be completed before access is granted to the prod environment.

3. Forward to the CAVP Program Manager your proof of completing the demo environment requirements. At this point, the CAVP Program Manager will check with NVLAP to see that step 1 has been completed. If so, prod credentials can be made and distributed for the applying 17ACVT laboratory.

4. The newly accredited 17ACVT laboratory must reach out to the CMVP Program Manager to obtain a CRADA (Cooperative Research and Development Agreement) for that financial year (October 1–September 30 the following calendar year). At this time, the CAVP will create a billing account for the newly accredited 17ACVT laboratory. Once the signed CRADA is verified, the production credentials will be distributed.

5.  The first requests the new laboratory should make are on the billing endpoints to request an allotment of vector sets for purchase. All labs must have an allotment of vector sets available in order to request vector sets to be generated. More information about the endpoints and purchases can be found on GitHub at `https://github.com/usnistgov/ACVP-Server`.

The estimated time to complete steps 1–3 is approximately two to four months. Much of the time depends on scheduling the on-site audit for the NVLAP accreditation process. The estimated time to complete step 4 is three to four business days if payment is made immediately after receiving the invoice.

# CHAPTER 7

# ACVTS Testing

The NIST CAVP (Cryptographic Algorithm Validation Program) utilizes the ACVTS (Automated Cryptographic Validation Test System). This is a set of programs and procedures for validating the implementation of approved cryptographic algorithms in order to support the certification for those implementations.

The CMVP maintains an online server that CST Labs can use to get test vectors and submit responses. This is the "automated" part of ACVTS. As a customer of NIST and a CST Lab, you will typically request vectors and receive them by email, then submit the responses back to the CST Lab by email. A CST Lab is free to implement whatever level of automation they choose for the interface between the CST Lab and the vendor.

The typical sequence between a vendor and a CST Lab is covered in detail in Chapter 6. But for convenience, a summary of the process flow is provided here:

1. The CST Lab sends demo vectors to the vendor. This is a JSON formatted file that contains the input vectors to the algorithm to be tested, along with a response file which gives the correct responses.

2. The vendor runs the vectors through their implementation to demonstrate to the CST Lab that the implementation correctly implements the algorithm specifications being tested against.

3. The vendor sends the generated demo responses back to the CST Lab.

4. In response to the vendor demonstrating they can correctly generate response vectors, the production vectors are sent to the vendor.

5. The vendor sends back the response vector generated by their implementation. The CST Lab submits the vectors and recommendation for certification to NIST.

© David Johnston and Richard Fant 2024
D. Johnston and R. Fant, *Designing to FIPS-140*, https://doi.org/10.1007/979-8-8688-0125-9_7

6. Assuming the vector responses were correct, an algorithm certificate will appear on the NIST website a few days later. This can take up to a week but is usually quicker.

To get the demo vectors and production vectors, the CST Lab is using the NIST ACVTS online portal. Vendors do not generally have access to this portal.

# 7.1 Vendor Information and Implementation Document

The communication channel between a vendor and their CST Lab for specific algorithm certification can take many forms. Some CST Labs use a simple Word document or Excel spreadsheet which the vendor fills in and then emails back. Other labs have online portals the vendor can use. One example online portal is the ACVTMate website provided by Atsec Corporation: `www.atsec.com/wp-content/uploads/2021/03/acvt_mate_01-1.html`.

While the information shared may vary a little between different CST Labs, typically the following information is supplied:

**Vendor Information**

Vendor Name: ACME Enterprises

Address: 123 Acme St,

City: Acmington,

State: Wyoming,

Zip Code: 45678

Country: USA

**Main Contact Info**

Contact Name: Wylie Coyote

Contact Email: WC@acme.com

Contact Phone: 123-456-7890

Contact Fax: 123-456-7891

Second Contact Info (if applicable):

Contact Name:

Contact Email:

Contact Phone:

Contact Fax:

The implementation name part contains the following fields:

**Implementation Details**

Implementation Name: CryptoThing

Software Version:

Part Number: CT2000

Firmware Version:

Implementation Type: Software/Firmware/**Hardware**

Processor (for Software/Firmware):

Operating System (for Software/Firmware):

Brief Implementation Description:

Request for Special Processing:

You may also get an ITAR option.

**ITAR**

This algorithm implementation is subject to the requirements of the US Department of State's International Traffic in Arms Regulations (ITAR). Yes/**No**.

The vendor's name, contact name, implementation names, and versions will all appear on the final certificate, which is publicly visible, so suitable forethought should be put into the contents of these fields. For the algorithm information, there are multiple algorithms and cipher options to choose from. Fill in the details for the algorithms that have been implemented and for which you are seeking certification.

# 7.2  Demo Vectors

The demo vectors are example vectors that can include the "answer sheet" (i.e., the correct response file). This can be used to check an implementation and the vector insertion and response extraction system.

Here are genuine demo vectors supplied from NIST for an RNG implementation using AES-128-CBC-MAC for the SP800-90B conditioner and AES-CTR-DRBG for the SP800-90A DRBG. Vectors for the underlying AES-128-ECB are also supplied.

Each set of vectors has a vsID, which is a unique number identifying the vector set. In this case, the vsID 802714 corresponds to the AES-ECB vector set, 802715 corresponds to the CTR-DRBG vector set, and 802716 corresponds to the CBC-MAC vector set.

In each vector set, there are two files: testvector-request.json and testvector-expected.json. The request file contains the input vectors. The expected file contains the expected response (i.e., "answer sheet").

# 7.2.1  AES-ECB Test Vector Request JSON

The file is large and repetitive, having 1536 lines of JSON, so a number of the test cases have been skipped in the following text.

The top-level structure of the file is a list of two things. The first is a structure with the acvVersion number as "1.0".

The second is the structure with everything else. It has a list of five things. The first four are the vsID, the algorithm name, the file revision which to date has always been "1.0", and the "isSample" setting.

The fifth and final element of the main structure is the testgroups structure which contains a list of testgroups. In this AES-ECB request file, there are six test groups. Each test group contains a list of tests of the same type. The standard specified two test types for AES-ECB are AFT and MCT (Monte Carlo).

For example, the first test group has the header

```
"tgId": 1,
        "testType": "AFT",
        "direction": "encrypt",
        "keyLen": 128,
        "tests": [
```

where "tgID" is the test group ID, "testType" is one of AFT or MCT, "direction" is encrypt or decrypt, and "keyLen" is 128, 192, or 256.

The last entry "tests" is the list of test cases within the test group. Each test case has a "tcID" (test case ID) number, a "pt" field containing the plaintext input to AES, and a "key" field containing the key input to AES.

You can see in the following tgID=5, the size of the plaintext field is increasing for each test case, starting at 128 bits and increasing by 128 bits for each subsequent test. This is not documented, but through trial and error it was established that what is intended is for the plaintext data to be chopped into 128-bit block and separately encrypted under the same key and the resulting outputs concatenated to make an output string of the same length as the input.

The "MCT" Monte Carlo test is documented in SP800-90B and involved 100,000 invocations of AES, iterating the input to the output with some XORing in between. In this request file, there is a single MCT test in tgID 6. The largest number of MCT test cases we have seen in a request file is 7, requiring 700,000 invocations of the AES unit. In software or direct test implementation in hardware, this is not a problem; however, it is a problem if the test vectors need to be passed in one by one into the hardware over JTAG (Joint Test Action Group - a standardized debug interface), where the bitrates are not fast. In one instance, the 700,000 iterations took 2 days to execute in the lab. The benefit of running so many iterations is questionable, and this presents a hardship on lab resources. NIST has not given a positive response to requests to reduce the iteration count.

```
[
  {
    "acvVersion": "1.0"
  },
  {
    "vsId": 802714,
    "algorithm": "ACVP-AES-ECB",
    "revision": "1.0",
    "isSample": true,
    "testGroups": [
      {
        "tgId": 1,
        "testType": "AFT",
        "direction": "encrypt",
        "keyLen": 128,
        "tests": [
          {
            "tcId": 1,
            "pt": "F34481EC3CC627BACD5DC3FB08F273E6",
            "key": "00000000000000000000000000000000"
          },
          {
            "tcId": 2,
            "pt": "9798C4640BAD75C7C3227DB910174E72",
            "key": "00000000000000000000000000000000"
          },
          {
            "tcId": 3,
            "pt": "9798C4640BAD75C7C3227DB910174E72",
            "key": "00000000000000000000000000000000"
          },
```

tcID 4-7 elided:

```
        ]
      },
      {
        "tgId": 2,
        "testType": "AFT",
        "direction": "encrypt",
        "keyLen": 128,
        "tests": [
          {
            "tcId": 8,
            "pt": "00000000000000000000000000000000",
            "key": "10A58869D74BE5A374CF867CFB473859"
          },
          {
            "tcId": 9,
            "pt": "00000000000000000000000000000000",
            "key": "CAEA65CDBB75E9169ECD22EBE6E54675"
          },
          {
            "tcId": 10,
            "pt": "00000000000000000000000000000000",
            "key": "A2E2FA9BAF7D20822CA9F0542F764A41"
          },
```

tcID 11-28 elided:

```
        ]
      },
      {
        "tgId": 3,
        "testType": "AFT",
        "direction": "encrypt",
        "keyLen": 128,
        "tests": [
          {
```

```
        "tcId": 29,
        "pt": "80000000000000000000000000000000",
        "key": "00000000000000000000000000000000"
    },
    {
        "tcId": 30,
        "pt": "C0000000000000000000000000000000",
        "key": "00000000000000000000000000000000"
    },
    {
        "tcId": 31,
        "pt": "E0000000000000000000000000000000",
        "key": "00000000000000000000000000000000"
    },
```

tcID 32-156 elided:

```
    ]
  },
  {
    "tgId": 4,
    "testType": "AFT",
    "direction": "encrypt",
    "keyLen": 128,
    "tests": [
      {
        "tcId": 157,
        "pt": "00000000000000000000000000000000",
        "key": "80000000000000000000000000000000"
      },
      {
        "tcId": 158,
        "pt": "00000000000000000000000000000000",
        "key": "C0000000000000000000000000000000"
      },
```

```
    {
      "tcId": 159,
      "pt": "00000000000000000000000000000000",
      "key": "F0000000000000000000000000000000"
    },
```

tcID 160-284 elided:

```
    ]
  },
  {
    "tgId": 5,
    "testType": "AFT",
    "direction": "encrypt",
    "keyLen": 128,
    "tests": [
      {
        "tcId": 285,
        "pt": "7E9E95F744F96925D1C05D42BAEBBDC3",
        "key": "FD44A5C5C5F9CB8606E42DCB1155C104"
      },
      {
        "tcId": 286,
        "pt": "1C0A3787DD8AB0AF1EED7D80FAE4E2A75EFF9040A719EFC9FDB40745
        590FE801",
        "key": "5543E86907CE37FD8BFE2901AE24A04C"
      },
      {
        "tcId": 287,
        "pt": "48ABE09C614ACFA4BD32CCEE59E3C70C5A9F79FA672CF04564B3682
        51A120FAF8F52D7E9B751087D91014964B14B0E4E",
        "key": "0396991D736CE75BE546638D32B7D8E0"
      },
      {
        "tcId": 288,
```

    "pt": "7A10EACA3533512003B336923B6B9F0BAB769E9DC31DE23239FEDE5
    6C48D39A8450103C5D4C33E1EB4EFD2BB77BE1889AEFB4B53DF65B87DD5BE8E
    7352060FD6",
    "key": "80172BB4D8458519AB5736BE1A3720B7"
},
{
    "tcId": 289,
    "pt": "DC1B5468070E9219FCFC19A0D98719611476325F4B2CA2F897A34D60
    C9C36926AEB209B041575540BABCA123795F772CDCE43EAC05C9C5E5CB95C05
    C4F4DD59D1F93FF51B3F5455322382810126D8E57",
    "key": "0E5B71748080C7D4DE7B1A7B42DF1A13"
},
{
    "tcId": 290,
    "pt": "94E726FDBE0EECDE8132F8DE227955F37DAD71708A618ADD8631FA8F
    4DA9387B0B05BFEE6F440127C05136BB187A1BDEDF5622A5EF262353D69642B
    F35AC30B7ED11593E5835499F536096ADB56074C8F1303C7D61268C65431723
    B9E4548856",
    "key": "B650C6D5303BF4E9E45009786C741A1D"
},
{
    "tcId": 291,
    "pt": "FD65F8D82ED3C31FD1FA70F7EEFD22B589D15BB37068089E30F3D065
    F9CE41B6B64B524EDA77D68AC1CF0770ECE849FC4A063ED2F4074450B4D3500
    55D85EED86A5CE038F96CBBC8A450BBB5B9BD7280F92DEAE8A7AB1396834CBB
    963F7BDA7D84C02D5F68422A35EEE67E079EC79C70",
    "key": "2E0E5E9E674DB8552CE50C70913D51F8"
},
{
    "tcId": 292,
    "pt": "705E40EE9D32D700165B3C79BC90224927C1D77EC50CCFAA7E1D6AD9
    73B0F2F8C236B4C5F2D6E32FD84262FD878F97D0C6CEF135C8A234242333C48
    061AF437958C4095360E91718F69F20F930F2DD439ECB88B6294ABCCC8A14AE
    0AEEDACFF93C93EF65D3369C4F851B80846EBE38D23EB35B30A87F0C4829DC8
    AFC399D3376248FB869C51BF7F9FC31363692E6A814",

```
          "key": "58597C552DDD107966ED5A4142CFDFFD"
        },
        {
          "tcId": 293,
          "pt": "9640139941BD84C7B831EAC16F1D2246DCDAD5E050E8E16D18DB92F
          2A08204FFBF21C6F7E8273735DFE7AB30B9F79683165882FB3269685C37FBC0
          78F363AE6462A3B805A1399E5ED6074AB8451869D95485564EE666A37826673
          087850D3D29A0F14923D0EA096CA76862D5E18FC367834685308C4E55ABC789
          F0AAA546C738DD2B480980ED1FD9B6E29D3B126A0116",
          "key": "60FE97C24F4CDEBAF123B700F732AA47"
        },
        {
          "tcId": 294,
          "pt": "BB909FFD7D534B9A9BB98F2368BCFF7DCB90D4B35248DC9CCFF4F50
          92A5059354654D6559F1A5FD22C2772BF3B476CE4ED0E5E1F4D25EF92E63F1
          7DC2577C10D78CB6AD4A1EC8C2AB022D842DAC2DBE6D11B80EC5ED200B1287
          7412B440FF404694D81172E3DFF6DFBBDF24DD61809286A5BEC197B2B5AFAE
          29911A05A87E7A2",
          "key": "FD78D529E39E7777EEE3E40DC617DE9B"
        }
      ]
    },
    {
      "tgId": 6,
      "testType": "MCT",
      "direction": "encrypt",
      "keyLen": 128,
      "tests": [
        {
          "tcId": 295,
          "pt": "506A741544AD2E7A368B94A926405E07",
          "key": "CB51EFB213A04F80A89B1E3EC92CA23E"
        }
      ]
    }
```

```
        ]
    }
]
```

## 7.2.2 Demo Vector Expected and Response JSON

The expected file delivered with demo vectors is the expected response to the input vectors in the request file. The vsID should match the vsID in the request file, and for each tgID and tcID in the request file, there will be a matching tgID and tcID in the expected file.

The following expected file is the file delivered with the demo vector set with vsID = 802714. For brevity, the same tcIDs (4-7, 11-28, 32-156, 160-284) have been removed as were removed in the request file.

The Monte Carlo test tgID=6, tcID=298, has a single input vector but generates 100 output vectors, 4 of which (the first and last 2) are shown in the following file:

```
[
  {
    "acvVersion": "1.0"
  },
  {
    "vsId": 802714,
    "algorithm": "ACVP-AES-ECB",
    "revision": "1.0",
    "isSample": true,
    "testGroups": [
      {
        "tgId": 1,
        "tests": [
          {
            "tcId": 1,
            "ct": "0336763E966D92595A567CC9CE537F5E"
          },
          {
            "tcId": 2,
```

```
          "ct": "A9A1631BF4996954EBC093957B234589"
        },
        {
          "tcId": 3,
          "ct": "A9A1631BF4996954EBC093957B234589"
        },
```

tcID 4-7 elided:

```
      ]
    },
    {
      "tgId": 2,
      "tests": [
        {
          "tcId": 8,
          "ct": "6D251E6944B051E04EAA6FB4DBF78465"
        },
        {
          "tcId": 9,
          "ct": "6E29201190152DF4EE058139DEF610BB"
        },
        {
          "tcId": 10,
          "ct": "C3B44B95D9D2F25670EEE9A0DE099FA3"
        },
```

tcID 11-28 elided:

```
      ]
    },
    {
      "tgId": 3,
      "tests": [
        {
          "tcId": 29,
          "ct": "3AD78E726C1EC02B7EBFE92B23D9EC34"
        },
```

```
    {
      "tcId": 30,
      "ct": "AAE5939C8EFDF2F04E60B9FE7117B2C2"
    },
    {
      "tcId": 31,
      "ct": "F031D4D74F5DCBF39DAAF8CA3AF6E527"
    },
```

tcID 32-156 elided:

```
    ]
  },
  {
    "tgId": 4,
    "tests": [
      {
        "tcId": 157,
        "ct": "0EDD33D3C621E546455BD8BA1418BEC8"
      },
      {
        "tcId": 158,
        "ct": "4BC3F883450C113C64CA42E1112A9E87"
      },
      {
        "tcId": 159,
        "ct": "970014D634E2B7650777E8E84D03CCD8"
      },
```

tcID 160-284 elided:

```
    ]
  },
  {
    "tgId": 5,
    "tests": [
      {
```

```
    "tcId": 285,
    "ct": "03EC89A5121473912CE78BB5D98C4A7A"
  },
  {
    "tcId": 286,
    "ct": "B46037526D9CF31688E8143D2046937F6101EF67EE610AA8ADF4A4B
    05F7618D3"
  },
  {
    "tcId": 287,
    "ct": "9AE6D6AA33FEC12BD8AD5500FB1208FFBCF4CB8BE300F1D74320800
    3D9DBD4BE6D00DEC4CF4993867A38644D3E66D756"
  },
  {
    "tcId": 288,
    "ct": "9086578B6C36BAF87E0EE2842B37F933F3C687C220C68FC0237C1675
    8FFA08EDD9166B08F03DFFFB8DC51F4BCD112908CCBC217C6C1627B133513F0
    950567F36"
  },
  {
    "tcId": 289,
    "ct": "DF04104E1808E54EA25F02B4CC4487A6A96B2D31A02B364B034082E2
    FDD7654EB4976B5A165FB72B1B5D7753453FAE4424DC13E68CA1D2A8CA4A7D9
    7235202515C861D59E32654F206F7D5861E1482B5"
  },
  {
    "tcId": 290,
    "ct": "F52B1FA219EF0280AC5BCD443FE0938ED42BC195911B66A0F90AD193
    3E61872BC76544F8C3C1AC571C061F96DDF61ECBE1B594C4F0074E6B2765617
    8173D6396DB5412753572E75BF99EAE976322C2AB104ABC397669F246E535F5
    5630C035FB"
  },
  {
    "tcId": 291,
```

```
      "ct": "A7437000DB8BAF4121E4C0497FC81F45132A472F41138B661CB58705
      4D13096D42890BF6DFD9D43D0FEDDE90F59A25FDF54CAE73D4DA73C9F0D645
      FDE5A4F8F540AA666129560CE4AF816C72D07CA21D601EE15CF2B4BD2568AF9
      E8A63DF3C3C951E37CED68104DAF0C4E4CEA48795CC"
    },
    {
      "tcId": 292,
      "ct": "5C2A104A1706DAC1B7DA8C5697618E290257186AFE1F401CF105FBCF
      DEE672C07441973A6C783EF52364E83CDA89D44501DF8EDE7922532CCC2712D
      9684088D55B11233335BC531FCCD4B0935A639F1817EC0E4D569857C583B6F6
      54319B294C29F7613330B255BBDB3A157DE9A21263617193D008B55D00806D8
      D12E1D0CF437869E25D6A8084C1A23839AAF1AD9377"
    },
    {
      "tcId": 293,
      "ct": "822EA86D3D0420F46C4846B9B616877095A039EF7AE84C574A68BD5
      C3B506A0ED002BF0360749739FC1DED349166052F4E4FCF5DAE710BD892D7A
      71108ACDA29E79E39DA0AA2FA0E9CE00616D81B7C8022F0CB035B43AC6EB1D
      996140B44B5C8E870B87E6348EAB8CBD7A9923A0EF048AC47EA583294B2F55
      BD4772375750E98D422C8344DD195EC779B03731309D8DE"
    },
    {
      "tcId": 294,
      "ct": "5E0324F0B5615D3BD4773FD655DFC6615E7938B09740A69E6E38D629
      2B5B9C1AAC46E8D6DA1E1F1E9FFA9393EB433FC2131981AB870EC10D4457581
      0937395C752DA93CE7FB33D2B66BAD9C32AB335B31936F9B78B926821630689
      049615E33DAE1B40847739674A5B2FA8912A74CFA921CDC4F207A013A0AC75
      A808967D4482"
    }
  ]
},
{
  "tgId": 6,
  "tests": [
```

```
{
  "tcId": 295,
  "resultsArray": [
    {
      "key": "CB51EFB213A04F80A89B1E3EC92CA23E",
      "pt": "506A741544AD2E7A368B94A926405E07",
      "ct": "BA03DBC87E30B97491CFBDA3EA500666"
    },
    {
      "key": "7152347A6D90F6F43954A39D237CA458",
      "pt": "BA03DBC87E30B97491CFBDA3EA500666",
      "ct": "95E60A206704CEEAC7A75E92F408086B"
    },
```

Middle 96 (2–98 of 100) results elided:

```
    {
      "key": "64BB24AC90C463BBB5FA3D64D9156125",
      "pt": "FA0A2CBB87DA81B927D467FBDF754C9A",
      "ct": "C209336F3518EA6BC3782A3AF5D4CE8C"
    },
    {
      "key": "A6B217C3A5DC89D07682175E2CC1AFA9",
      "pt": "C209336F3518EA6BC3782A3AF5D4CE8C",
      "ct": "483D89F4E5C2573554D0C974091B087C"
    }
  ]
}
  ]
}
  ]
}
]
```

# 7.2.3 **Reading ACVTS Request Files**

The AES-ECB test example requests file loads as a list of two dictionaries. The first dictionary contains a single element with the acvVersion value. The second list element is a dictionary with the test settings and the testGroups structure.

The following code will load the AES-ECB request file and extract the tests, which will be one of AFT encrypt, AFT decrypt, MCT encrypt, or MCT decrypt, along with one of three key sizes and variable-length plaintext and ciphertext blocks in the AFT tests.

In the python code that this is derived from, the printout section instead sends the vectors to the implementation. In your own testing, the particulars of how to send the vectors into the implementation will depend on your design.

```python
def aes_ecb_acvt_reader(filename):
    testgroups = list()
    with open(filename,"r") as cavsjson:
        challenge = json.load(filename)

    acvversion  = challenge[0]["acvVersion"]
    testgroups  = challenge[1]["testGroups"]
    issample    = challenge[1]["isSample"]
    algorithm   = challenge[1]["algorithm"]
    vsId        = challenge[1]["vsId"]
    revision    = challenge[1]["revision"]

    print("acvVersion = ",acvversion)
    print("isSample   = ",isSample)
    print("algorithm  = ",algorithm)
    print("vsID       = ",vsId)
    print("revision   = ",revision)

    # Iterate through the test groups
    for testgroup in testgroups:
        tgid      = testgroup["tgId"]
        keylen    = testgroup["keyLen"]
        direction = testgroups["direction"]
        testtype  = testgroups["testType"]
        tests     = testgroups["tests"]
```

```
# Iterate through the tests in the test group
# If the direction is 'encrypt' expect key and pt.
# If the direction is 'decrypt' expect key and ct.
# Each test is a dictionary
for testdict in tests:
    tcid = int(testdict[u'tcID'])
    key  = int(testdict[u'key'])

    if testtype = "AFT" and direction=="encrypt":
        print("AFT Encryption Test")
        print(" tgID ",tgid)
        print(" tcID ",tcid)
        if keyLen==128:
            print("Key = 0x%032x", key)
        elif keyLen==192:
            print("Key = 0x%048x", key)
        elif keyLen==256:
            print("Key = 0x%064x", key)
        # plaintext can be multiple blocks
        pt   = testdict[u'pt']
        num_blocks = int(len(pt)/32)

        if num_blocks == 1:
            print("Plaintext = 0x032x",pt)
        else:
            for i in range(num_blocks):
                ptb = int(pt[i*32:(i+1)*32],16)
                print("block %s : 0x%032x" % (i,ptb))

    elif testtype == "AFT" and direction=="decrypt":
        print("AFT Decryption Test")
        print(" tgID ",tgid)
        print(" tcID ",tcid)
        if keyLen==128:
            print("Key = 0x%032x", key)
        elif keyLen==192:
            print("Key = 0x%048x", key)
        elif keyLen==256:
```

```python
        print("Key = 0x%064x", key)
    # ciphertext can be multiple blocks
    ct   = testdict[u'ct']
    num_blocks = int(len(pt)/32)

    if num_blocks == 1:
        print("Ciphertext = 0x%s" % pt)
    else:
        for i in range(num_blocks):
            ctb = int(ct[i*32:(i+1)*32],16)
            print("block %s : 0x%032x" % (i,ptb))

elif testtype == "MCT" and direction=="encrypt":
    print("MCT Encryption Test")
    print(" tgID ",tgid)
    print(" tcID ",tcid)
    if keyLen==128:
        print("Key = 0x%032x", key)
    elif keyLen==192:
        print("Key = 0x%048x", key)
    elif keyLen==256:
        print("Key = 0x%064x", key)
    pt   = int(testdict[u'pt'],16)
    print("Plaintext = 0x%s" % pt)

elif testtype == "MCT" and direction=="decrypt":
    print("MCT Decryption Test")
    print(" tgID ",tgid)
    print(" tcID ",tcid)
    if keyLen==128:
        print("Key = 0x%032x", key)
    elif keyLen==192:
        print("Key = 0x%048x", key)
    elif keyLen==256:
        print("Key = 0x%064x", key)
    ct   = int(testdict[u'ct'],16)
    print("Ciphertext = 0x%s" % pt)
```

# 7.2.4  Comparing ACVTS Expected and Response JSON Files

When a response JSON file is generated, it should logically match the expected JSON file. This does not mean that the order of entries in a list or the whitespace in the file needs to match, but the structure and content of the tuple pairs and lists must match exactly.

For example:

```
{
    "vsId": 802714,
    "algorithm": "ACVP-AES-ECB",
    "revision": "1.0",
    "isSample": true,
    "testGroups": [...]
}
```

is logically identical to the following with different whitespace and different ordering of key-value tuples:

```
{
"revision": "1.0",
"isSample": true,
"vsId": 802714,
"algorithm": "ACVP-AES-ECB",
"testGroups": [...]
}
```

JSON libraries will correctly make this comparison. In the following code, the python 3 JSON library example is used to read two files, and they are compared for logical equality:

```
import json
def compare_acvt_responses(filename1, filename2):
    with open(filename1, "r") as cavsjson:
        challenge1 = json.load(cavsjson)
    with open(filename2, "r") as cavsjson:
        challenge2 = json.load(cavsjson)
    return (challenge1==challenge2)
```

# 7.3  Other JSON Schema for ACVP

The preceding AES-ECB examples cover only one of the schema specified in the ACVP program. The schema are defined as Internet drafts. The primary NIST page for ACVP schema is at https://pages.nist.gov/ACVP where there are currently links to 200 schema covering all the algorithms within the ACVP program.

# 7.4  Example of a Real ACVP Certificate

A certificate for the algorithms in an Intel RNG in the Skylake Xeon 28 core die can be seen at the following URL: https://csrc.nist.gov/projects/cryptographic-algorithm-validation-program/details?product=14291.

The certificate headings contain information submitted to the CST Lab through the JSON form. In this instance, the version information is moot. The "version" is the version of the DRNG that was specifically designed for the Xeon Skylake series and is baked into silicon. It does not change. In the case of software libraries, the version numbering is important and must uniquely identify the version of the software implementing the algorithms.

| Implementation Name | Intel DRNG (DRNG) | | |
|---|---|---|---|
| Description | Intel Digital Random Number Generator with SP800-90A AES128-CTR-DRBG and SP800-90B noise source with AES128-CBC-MAC Vetted Conditioning Component | | |
| Version | DRNG-Server-Coop | | |
| Type | HARDWARE | | |
| Vendor | Intel Corporation 2200 Mission College Blvd Santa Clara , CA 95054 USA | Contacts | David Johnston dj.johnston@intel.com +1-503-261-3658 |

***Figure 7-1.***  *Skylake-28 DRNG Algorithm Certificate Vendor Information Header*

The RNG contains AES which is used for an SP800-90B CBC-MAC conditioner and a CTR-DRBG. Therefore, three algorithms are certified – AES-ECB, CTR-DRBG, and CBC-MAC.

**A1791**  First Validated: 8/3/2021     | Collapsed | Expanded | Aggregated |

| Operating Environment | Algorithm Capabilities |
|---|---|
| Intel Corporation Intel(R) Xeon(R) Skylake-28 FCLGA3647 Intel(R) Xeon(R) Platinum 8276CL Processor   ⊕ | **AES-ECB**   ⊕ |
| Intel Corporation Intel(R) Xeon(R) Skylake-28 FCLGA3647 Intel(R) Xeon(R) Platinum 8276CL Processor   ⊕ | **Conditioning Component AES-CBC-MAC SP800-90B**   ⊕ |
| Intel Corporation Intel(R) Xeon(R) Skylake-28 FCLGA3647 Intel(R) Xeon(R) Platinum 8276CL Processor   ⊕ | **Counter DRBG**   ⊕ |

***Figure 7-2.**  Skylake-28 DRNG Algorithm Certificates*

The A-number A1791 identifies the certificate set for the RNG. The entries in the Algorithm Capabilities column can be expanded to show the parameters of the algorithm that was tested. In this case, the RNG is a shared RNG serving all the cores, and so DRBG optional features like nonces, additional input, and personalization strings are not implemented.

**Counter DRBG**   ⊖

Prediction Resistance: No
Supports Reseed
Capabilities:
    Mode: AES-128
    Derivation Function Enabled: No
    Additional Input: 0
    Entropy Input: 256
    Nonce: 0
    Personalization String Length: 0
    Returned Bits: 128

***Figure 7-3.**  Skylake-28 Expanded CTR-DRBG Algorithm Certificate Information*

# CHAPTER 8

# Entropy Assessment

## 8.1 What Is Entropy?

Entropy is commonly referred to as a measure of disorder or information capacity of a communication channel. Entropy as defined by Alfréd Rényi is called Rényi Entropy with a parameter alpha. There are an infinite number of entropy measures based on that value that can take on any nonnegative real value. The equation is

$$H_\alpha(X) = H_\alpha(p_1,\ldots,p_n) = \frac{1}{1-\alpha}\log_2\left(\sum_{i=1}^{n}P_i^\alpha\right), \alpha \geq 0, \alpha \neq 1$$

**H** is the symbol for entropy. **X** is the symbol for the distribution from which random symbols are drawn. **$p_i$** is the probability of the $i^{th}$ symbol from the distribution of

$$X = \{p1, p2, , pn\}.$$

When relating this to an entropy source design, you can consider the distribution of the symbols outputted from the entropy source. Rényi entropy gives a measure of entropy as a function of that distribution.

Rényi entropy with $\alpha = 0$ is called max entropy or Hartley entropy, and it assumes all symbols are equiprobable. For a distribution of n distinct values, the max entropy is $-\log_2(n)$. For example, a uniform random byte has 256 distinct values, meaning n = 256, and the max entropy would be $H_0 = \log_2(256) = 8$ bits. It should not come as a surprise that there are at most 8 bits of entropy in a byte of data.

Rényi entropy with $\alpha = 1$ is called Shannon entropy. This is the information capacity form that is used in physics, communications, and information theory. It can be seen as the weighted average of the entropy of all the symbols. Since the parametric equation reduces to $\frac{0}{0}$ when $\alpha = 1$, we must instead take a limit to compute the Shannon entropy, and after some effort, we arrive at

© David Johnston and Richard Fant 2024
D. Johnston and R. Fant, *Designing to FIPS-140*, https://doi.org/10.1007/979-8-8688-0125-9_8

$$H_1(X) = H_1(p_1,\ldots,p_n) = -\sum_{i=1}^{n} p_i \log_2(p_i)$$

Rényi entropy with $\alpha = 2$ is called collision entropy. Given two independent and identically distributed random variables **X** and **Y**, the collision entropy is the negative log of the probability of variables drawn from **X** and **Y** being equal.

$$H_2(X) = H_2(p_1,\ldots,p_n) = -\log_2 \sum_{i=1}^{n} p_i^2 = -\log_2 P(X = Y)$$

The most conservative measure of entropy is called min-entropy. It is a function of the probability of the optimal guess for a value drawn from a distribution. Accordingly, it is computed as

$$H_\infty(X) = H_\infty(p_1,\ldots,p_n) = -\log_2\left(max(p_i)\right)$$

where P(xi) is the probability of each symbol drawn from a set of symbols in the distribution X.

In the FIPS certification context and cryptographic context in general, entropy is always measured in terms of min-entropy. Given a PMF (Probability Mass Function) which is the distribution of a finite set of symbols, the min-entropy is simply the negative log base 2 of the probability of the highest point in the distribution. In the distribution in Figure 8-1, we have sampled a space of nonuniform random digits between 1 and 16. The y axis gives the probabilities of each symbol occurring based on the sample results. We can see that 9 is the most probable, with an individual probability of 0.1072319. The min-entropy can be computed to be close to $-\log_2(0.1072319) = 3.221$ bits. Since 4 bits are required to represent numbers between 1 and 16, this means we have an entropy rate of $\dfrac{3.221}{4} = 0.805$.

If you made a guess of what symbol would be drawn from the distribution, your best choice would be the peak of the distribution. If you were guessing a cryptographic key, you would guess the value with the highest probability. So, the min-entropy is a measure of how hard it is to guess a key. Min-entropy is the primary form of entropy used in cryptography.

Unless otherwise stated, "entropy" in this book refers to "min-entropy."

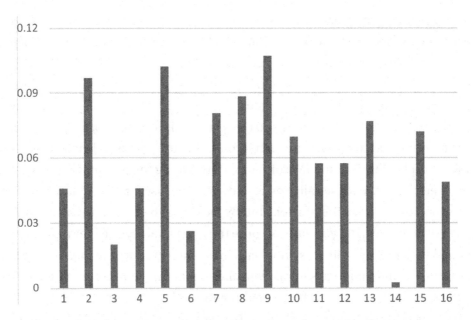

***Figure 8-1.*** *Probability Mass Function Histogram for a Distribution*

# 8.2  Measuring Entropy of Finite Binary Sequences

In the real world, infinite binary sequences are not possible to generate, and without perfect knowledge of the construction of the noise source and the environment around it, it is generally impossible to perfectly know the entropy of the data that would come from it. Thus, we have to approximate with measurements over finite amounts of data sampled from the source. Also, we can build mathematical models of the noise source and run simulations. When there is good correspondence between the three results from measurement, simulation, and modeling, it can be inferred that the measurements are close to the true value.

For the measurement of entropy from data, we need enough data that the measurement algorithms can produce a repeatable result. They do not in general produce a reliable result as we will see when we compare the performance of SP800-90B Non-IID tests against model data with known entropy.

For a simple example, binary data from a noise source which makes unbiased bits but has high positive serial correlation might turn out to be

0000000000000000000001111111111111111111111

Measuring the mean over all those bits gives you an optimal mean of 0.5. Measuring the mean over the first 20 bits 00000000000000000000 gives a worst-case mean of 0 and a serial correlation of 0, which is as wrong as it could be.

If you were to make a naïve entropy analysis, you might observe that the symbol size is 2 since the symbol set is 0, 1 for binary bits. The distribution p0, p1 measured from the data 0.5, 0.5 since the zeroes and ones are equiprobable. So, the min-entropy would be computed as $\log_2(0.5) = 1$ which implies that the data is full entropy. It clearly is not full entropy. This discrepancy comes from assuming the distribution is static for each bit when it is not. With serially correlated data, the distribution of outcome of a bit depends on the value of the previous bit. By looking at bit pairs and calculating the total mean over all the data, you can compute the most likely symbol for many bits and the probability of that most likely symbol and from that compute the min-entropy. It is important to both have enough sample data and to make the entropy analysis over all the data, taking the relationships between the symbols into account.

When measuring the entropy of binary data, you must have enough data in order to get an accurate estimate of the min-entropy. With too little data, as seen previously, you can get a very wrong result.

You must also use correct metrics. Simply measuring the mean is usually not enough to determine the entropy.

# 8.3 Entropy of Non-full Entropy and Non-IID Binary Sequences

The physical processes that generate bits from environmental noise, typically electrical noise, always generate bits that are not full entropy. The physical process will introduce some statistical non-uniformity to the data it produces. The most common and simply defined statistical defects are bias and serial correlation. We can mathematically derive the entropy for data with these properties.

For biased data, the probability $P(1)$ is the probability of getting a 1 and $P(0)$ the probability of getting a 0. $P(1) + P(0) = 1$, since a 1 or a 0 is the only possible outcome. Full entropy binary data will always have the uniform distribution $P(1) = P(0) = 0.5$. For non-full entropy that is biased but with no serial correlation or other defects has the min-entropy of a distribution $X = P(1), P(0)$ as

$$H_\infty(X) = -\log_2\big(max\big(P(1), P(0)\big)\big)$$

For example, with P(1) = 0.3 and P(0) = 0.7, on average there would be 30% ones and 70% zeroes in the data. 1KiByte of such data, in hex, might look like this, with the majority of hex digits containing only 0 or 1 set bits, such as 0, 2, 4, or 8:

```
$ djenrandom -m biased --bias=0.3
44D400A140A2046B420674240252182E0026A8100801AC0527D8040418685118
40424AAD006870459343083CC1348C2010491338C1A862809A04A88014120801
82D0802039A5703505800A55802219408A0C81CE8120308805440040342F018A
6889028186005013F80027E5C3D12072E00C0041000E804B4021005201910801
C40842982A54903A08CC0115558280200511700222020460A63040988062031
8244201040140802461AC13040C000211C6F590000489028648800E9B20108A
0C6089800000C821284120A0161010430209C42060590C08E0011C0CD201D0F6
121200322352000205764210E80828315830F11712200020A37008480734800
010A2131D45801000AB81A660950018442B2002018F02304932D4D108478CE22
8820072414820083310369300B4004A934069846400040250B1142C6A644468
203144C008C40F02A4009C444C0D182130030E10600240181427B0220A490530
00D084898E0020201713CC9C202C4A24C40544D32804580D474980A0624A40B5
212544A080300C064C10022689086402808648807008529192600404041220
7092E9AD010B08EA221CF09340C940164183845C20035484E78BC8EA108A0005
A28806EA06452045301741CD8637106121208A3BD4052550D21B259170016011
7A9768821164E935E05A0116824D354130262945A004814C411313044C2120AC
89084421036035C100640898260C2A52121F07000204014E2510DCC9B8CC35F8
19312084250F3454A30C0A802C0B40A811C350521018211035487011CA9300800
700811C00131228317600C1C180014812428744C0853140F4190010CA4110178
10C40B04CA2C4086852B00806CB4CA5120D2450800A088803BA40449829DA4E1
254C020040B12348B10A1069408007040221B0A6800022888004310C8388F654
741180841878B180270280A202BDC180618AC490088000C00002433132F438A0
56040D285021BB810691CC8D220EE23114A2443002CC4400F3D1B3005171BD60
C550048111481A440A52865234B4C84AE5488012328708B4B13C2B4014786798
2C32A22284FA466211400509D0D00DC4A0D000D2A2044A0154549C8A4BE88296
A9A14E81CCC040154A48ACA08418B7026F00233440C1A69C2504271034690018
120951C268586694F5006104DC40CE0D81A8ABA21B40C0C8C2C121C001901A44
01F04312A818C38140104C810590A30200E48BCA43E801412267A5AC289562F0
69017683621905000049402008A1109D5002440D11022E4410144E4C40020B144
4864CA104A001A12520885C13568160816D00C7002142000121FD0135D4C2222
130053964A46A424740900A8618836139A0809060A0C00840081144001283804
834440A0580104AE0146805051578082C24880812208A4488C8AD08060130A56
```

Figure 8-2 shows a plot of min-entropy per bit vs. bias of the data, and we get a convex curve with the maximum at $P(1) = P(0) = 0.5$.

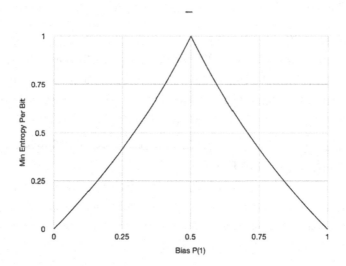

**Figure 8-2.** *Min-Entropy Variation with Bias*

The SCC (serial correlation coefficient) is a measure of the tendency of a bit to be the same or different from the previous bit. The range of SCC (serial correlation coefficient) is from $-1$ to $+1$. A value of SCC $= 0$ indicates there is no serial correlation. A value of SCC $= -1$ means that each bit is the inverse of the previous (0101010...). A value of SCC $= +1$ means that each bit is the same as the next (111111... or 000000...). The full equation for the correlation coefficient c between two data sequences $x = x_0, x_1...x_{n-1}$ and $y = y_0, y_1...y_{n-1}$ is

$$c = \frac{n\left(\sum_{i=0}^{n-1} x_i y_i\right) - \left(\sum_{i=0}^{n-1} x_i\right)\left(\sum_{i=0}^{n-1} y_i\right)}{\sqrt{\left(n\sum_{i=0}^{n-1} x_i^2 - \left(\sum_{i=0}^{n-1} x_i\right)^2\right)\left(n\sum_{i=0}^{n-1} y_i^2 - \left(\sum_{i=0}^{n-1} y_i\right)^2\right)}}$$

Substituting $x_{i+1 \bmod n}$ for $y_i$ gives the serial correlation coefficient, or SCC:

$$scc = \frac{n\left(\sum_{i=0}^{n-1} x_i x_{(i+1 \bmod n)}\right) - \left(\sum_{i=0}^{n-1} x_i\right)^2}{n\left(\sum_{i=0}^{n-1} x_i^2\right) - \left(\sum_{i=0}^{n-1} x_i\right)^2}$$

When the elements of x are all binary, the equation simplifies. Also, the mod $n$ treats the data as being cyclical, which with time series data is wrong. So reducing n to n − 1 and counting the number of set bits over the first n − 1 bits yields a simpler equation for SCC over binary data. count00, count01, count10, and count11 are the counts of all four two-bit patterns within the data.

The 2-bit pattern counts include overlapping pairs. For example, count11 over the 4-bit sequence 1111 would be 3 for the 3-bit positions where 11 can be found:

[11]11

1[11]1

11[11]

The count of 2-bit values is n-1 since there are only n-1 places to put two adjacent bits in n bits. The SCC using these counts simplifies to

$$n-1 = count00 + count01 + count10 + count11$$

$$scc = \frac{(n-1)count11 - (count01 + count11)(count01 + count11)}{(n-1)(count01 + count11) - (count01 + count11)(count01 + count11)}$$

Defining count1 = count01 + count11, the SCC simplifies to

$$scc = \frac{(n-1)count11 - count1^2}{(n-1)count1 - count1^2}$$

So, we have simple methods for measuring the bias and serial correlation coefficient within finite binary data strings by counting the number of 1s and the number of 11 bit pairs.

With positive SCC and no bias, the most common value for any string of n bits is 000000… or 11111….

With negative SCC and no bias, the most common value for any string of n bits is alternating 010101… or 101010….

With unbiased but serially correlated data, there is a simpler equation for the SCC:

$$scc = 2P(x_i = x_{i+1}) - 1$$

The per-bit min-entropy of such data is

$$H_\infty(X|SCC = s) = -log_2\left(max\left(\left(\frac{s}{2} + 0.5\right), 1 - \left(\frac{s}{2} + 0.5\right)\right)\right)$$

Figure 8-3 shows a plot of min-entropy against serial correlation.

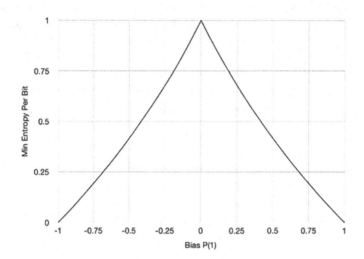

***Figure 8-3.*** *Min-Entropy Variation of Unbiased, Serially Correlated Data*

Where there is both bias and serial correlation, the derivation of min-entropy is more complicated and outside the scope of this book. The summary is that SCC and bias can be converted to a pair of transition probabilities on a two-state Markov generator which would generate data with that SCC and bias. From the Markov generator, we can derive the maximum probability symbol for a given bit width and so derive the min-entropy.

A python library to perform this analysis is available at

https://github.com/dj-on-github/markov2p

In the following python session, the library is imported, and a pair of transition probabilities is calculated from a bias of 0.4 and SCC of –0.2. The transition probabilities are used to compute the min-entropy per bit for groups of 8 bits.

```
>>> import markov2p
>>> p01,p10 = markov2p.biasscc_2_p(0.4,-0.2)
>>> h,_,_ = markov2p.p_to_entropy(p01,p10,8)
>>> h
mpfr('0.78485708872447227')
```

So, the min-entropy per bit, when looking at groups of 8 bits from the source with a bias of 0.4 and SCC of –0.2, is approximately 0.784.

The entropy for smaller groups of bits is higher, since this is assuming the state of the first bit is not known, and so its contribution to the total entropy is higher than for other bits for which the previous bit imparts some information.

For example, in an 8-bit sequence x, from a source with bias, scc = 0.4, –0.2, and $x = \{x_0, x_1, ..., x_7\}$. The first bit $x_0$ was preceded by unknown data. The distribution of the first bit is determined by the bias only. The remaining 7 bits $x_1, ..., x_7$ each have a distribution that is a function of the previous bit, the SCC and the bias.

If you were modeling a source this way, in order to feed 1024 bits of entropic data into a conditioner, you would want to compute using a group size of 1024.

We can see that with the larger bit width the min-entropy has gone from 0.784 to 0.766. This kind of analysis is useful when trying to determine the actual entropy and compare it against measured data and simulation. It can also form part of an analysis in an entropy justification report. However, it will not contribute to the assessed entropy, which is strictly determined from the non-IID or IID tests, the restart tests, and $H_{submitter}$ discussed in greater detail in Section 8.6.

In SP800-90B, there are a variety of H numbers: $H_{submitter}$, $H_{original}$, $H_r$, $H_c$, $H_{bitstring}$, and $H_{initial}$. The final assessed entropy is a function of the H numbers and the entropy test results.

# 8.4  MCV Entropy Analysis

MCV (most common value) entropy analysis measures entropy by simply counting the frequency of symbols of data to find $max(p_i)$ from which to calculate the min-entropy with the min-entropy formula from Section 8.1.

$$H_\infty(X) = -log_2\left(\max_i(p_i)\right)$$

Taking the MCV of 1-bit symbols is not useful for data with serial correlation since it takes into account only the bias. MCV analysis of multi-bit symbols will yield a distribution that is influenced by the serial correlation as well as the bias. The more bits per symbol, the better. However, at the other extreme, counting symbols with too many bits (e.g., 64-bit values) will not yield a useful distribution, since it would take too much data to yield a representative distribution. Performing MCV analysis at 8 or 16 bits is effective for computing an approximate min-entropy.

The djent program will compute the MCV entropy of data. The following djent is being used to measure the MCV entropy over 8-bit symbols in a 10MiByte file:

```
$ djenrandom -s -k 10240 -m markov_2_param --bias=0.4 --correlation=-0.2 -b
> rand.bin
$ djent -b -l 8 rand.bin | grep Min
```

```
  Min Entropy (by max occurrence of symbol 2a) = 0.784586
```

Measuring at symbol sizes from 1 to 16 bits shows how the measured entropy approaches the actual min-entropy of around 0.78, with increasing symbol size but then starts to underestimate the min-entropy as the symbol size gets too large.

| Symbol Size | MCV Min-Entropy per Bit |
|-------------|-------------------------|
| 1           | 0.737094                |
| 2           | 0.840324                |
| 3           | 0.756466                |
| 4           | 0.803265                |
| 5           | 0.759964                |
| 6           | 0.790709                |
| 7           | 0.762315                |
| 8           | 0.784586                |
| 9           | 0.723000                |
| 10          | 0.721741                |
| 11          | 0.685378                |
| 12          | 0.633856                |
| 13          | 0.638313                |
| 14          | 0.614721                |
| 15          | 0.567098                |
| 16          | 0.562412                |

# 8.5  Actual Min-Entropy vs. Lower Bound Min-Entropy

The preceding measurement types give an approximation to the actual min-entropy of data from a noise source. With increasing data size, the accuracy of the estimate increases.

The following procedures are those defined in SP800-90B and give a "lower bound" for the min-entropy. This is a value that is claimed to be below the actual entropy. So with the lower bound estimate from the SP800-90B algorithms, it is possible to make a claim that the actual min-entropy is above the lower bound, without specifying an actual min-entropy.

A heuristic analysis for the min-entropy of a source should usually yield a value higher than the SP800-90B lower bound estimate. In practice, the SP800-90B algorithms are not perfect and can both overestimate and underestimate the lower bound of the min-entropy of data from a noise source.

# 8.6  IID vs. Non-IID

IID stands for Independent and Identically Distributed.

The identically distributed part means that for each symbol, the distribution is the same and not changing over time. Data with serial correlation or any other form of dependence between bits inevitably leads to the distribution changing between bits, and so the identically distributed requirement isn't met. In random number generators (RNG) built into computers, we usually are dealing with sources that generate single bit symbols in a bit stream. Each bit must have the same distribution. This will be given by the probabilities {p0, p1} of the two symbols, where p0 + p1 = 1.

The independent part seems to derive from the identically distributed part. If each symbol is drawn from the same distribution, then they cannot be dependent.

However, the currently known laws of physics do not permit a process to exist which can create non-IID data from interacting (entangled) particles. One aspect of entanglement is that it is the process of putting particles into correlated states. In addition, current extractor theory, a mathematical discipline in computer science, has proofs that without a seed source of IID data, you cannot generate more IID data. So you could argue that you should not be allowed to claim that your entropy source provides IID data. You may be able to get very close to IID with good engineering, and it may be so close to IID that may be indistinguishable from truly IID data. The rules for determining if the testing is going to follow the IID track or non-IID track are in SP800-90B Section 3.1.2:

1. The submitter makes an IID claim on the noise source, based on the submitter's analysis of the design. The submitter **shall** provide rationale for the IID claim.

2. The sequential dataset described in item 1 of Section 3.1.1 is tested using the statistical tests described in Section 5 to verify the IID assumption, and the IID assumption is verified (i.e., there is no evidence that the data is not IID).

3. The row and column datasets described in item 3 of Section 3.1.1 are tested using the statistical tests described in Section 5 to verify the IID assumption, and the IID assumption is verified.

4. If a conditioning component that is not listed in Section 3.1.5.1.1 is used, the conditioned sequential dataset (described in item 2 of Section 3.1.1) is tested using the statistical tests described in Section 5 to verify the IID assumption, and the IID assumption is verified.

If you go through the certification process claiming you have an IID source, you should expect skepticism about the claim and expect to receive detailed scrutiny of your analysis from the CMVP. Your heuristic analysis would need to be watertight, along with all the statistical testing being thorough. Even if you think you have an IID source, it would be simpler to prove you are achieving some high entropy above some bound such as an entropy rate of 0.9 and use the non-IID track. Some in the industry, including the authors of this book, have called for the IID track to be removed.

The statistical tests in the SP800-90B Section 5 "Testing the IID Assumption" include two test types, permutation testing with 11 specific test algorithms in 5.1.1 through to 5.1.11 and Chi-Square testing with 5 specific test algorithms in 5.2.1 through 5.2.5.

## 8.6.1 Permutation Testing

Permutation testing creates 10,000 permutations of the test data and runs the data through the 11 tests. Each test creates a test statistic, and these statistics should not change significantly if the data is close enough to IID. In Section 5.1, the top-level permutation procedure is given in pseudocode:

```
Input: S = (s₁,..., s_L)
Output: Decision on the IID assumption
1. For each test i
   1.1. Assign the counters C_{i,0} and C_{i,1} to zero.
   1.2. Calculate the test statistic T_i on S.
2. For j = 1 to 10 000
   2.1. Permute S using the Fisher-Yates shuffle algorithm.
   2.2. For each test i
      2.2.1.  Calculate the test statistic T on the permuted data.
      2.2.2.  If (T > T_i), increment C_{i,0}. If (T = T_i), increment C_{i,1}.
3. If ((C_{i,0}+C_{i,1}≤5) or (C_{i,0}≥9995)) for any i, reject the IID
assumption; else, assume that the noise source outputs are IID.
```

These tests can be run using the ea_iid tool described in Section 8.9.7.

# 8.7  H Numbers and Assessed Entropy

$H_{submitter}$ is a claimed number for the entropy of data from the noise source, based on a heuristic analysis and testing by the submitter. The heuristic analysis should be included in the SP800-90B compliance document. This will in general be either a number close to the actual entropy or a number below the actual entropy that has a comfortable margin. For example, an entropy source might be reliably generating entropy in the 0.75–0.85 range but varies from product to product. The submitter may enter an $H_{submitter}$ value of 0.7 as a claim that the entropy from the source is always at least 0.7, and 0.7 bits of entropy per bit can be relied upon.

Typically, if a conservative value for $H_{submitter}$ has been given, the $H_{submitter}$ will be lower than $H_{original}$ or $H_{bitstring}$ and so will determine the assessed entropy. If the $H_{submitter}$ is set to a realistic number for the entropy of the source, the resulting assessed entropy will be lower as a result of the SP800-90B Section 6 tests being lower bound tests rather than accurate tests. The tests claim to deliver a number that is guaranteed to be lower than the actual entropy. However, it is good practice to set $H_{submitter}$ to be lower than the measured entropy and design the conditioner parameters to tolerate an input entropy rate lower than $H_{submitter}$ and lower than the health test cutoff entropy levels, so that the health tests fail before unacceptable low-quality entropy is passed to the conditioner marked as good entropy.

## 8.7.1  $H_{original}$

$H_{original}$ is the result from the SP800-90B entropy assessment tests, either the IID test in SP800-90B 6.1 or the lowest result from the non-IID tests in SP800-90B 6.2, depending on which track (IID or non-IID) is followed.

## 8.7.2  $H_{bitstring}$

When the non-IID tests are run on symbols that are larger than a single bit, the tests are run both on those symbols and over a bitstring that is generated by converting the multi-bit symbols to a string of single bits.

$H_{bitstring}$ is the result of the non-IID tests run over the bitstring data.

## 8.7.3  $H_{initial}$

Provided the noise source is producing multi-bit symbols, $H_{initial}$ is defined as

$$H_{initial} = min(H_{original}, H_{bitstring}, H_{submitter})$$

If the noise source produces single-bit symbols, $H_{original} = H_{bitstring}$, and in the flow of the document, there is no $H_{bitstring}$. In this case, $H_{initial}$ is defined as

$$H_{initial} = min(H_{original}, H_{submitter})$$

$H_{initial}$ is therefore the lower of the entropy test result and the $H_{submitter}$ claim you make.

## 8.7.4  $H_r$, $H_c$

Restart testing takes 1000 files of 1000 bits collected over 1000 restarts of the noise source. The data is arranged into a matrix of 1000 rows by 1000 columns.

$H_r$ is the SP800-90B Section 6 (6.1 or 6.2) test result over the restart data arranged by row.

$H_c$ is the SP800-90B Section 6 (6.1 or 6.2) test result over the restart data arranged by column.

The pass/fail rule for restart testing is if the sanity check passes and $min(H_r, H_c) \geq \left(\frac{1}{2}\right) H_{initial}$, then the restart test passes and $H = min(H_r, H_c, H_{initial})$.

## 8.7.5  Assessed Entropy

Assessed entropy is $\min(H_r, H_c, H_{initial})$. This is the final entropy result for the noise source. The primary goal of the SP800-90B noise source analysis is to show that the assessed entropy rate is greater than or equal to the claimed $H_{min}$ made by the designer. This claimed rate must satisfy the minimum required entropy rate into the conditioning component in order to achieve full entropy out from the conditioning component.

## 8.7.6  Choosing H Numbers and Setting Test Thresholds

When designing an RNG for a system that is to be certified against SP800-90B, there is a circular dependency between the assessed entropy, the health test entropy cutoffs, the $H_{submitter}$ value you claim, and the RNG design.

You cannot calculate the assessed entropy until you have built the RNG. The RNG design includes the extractor ratio and the cutoff values computed from the RCT (Repetition Count Test) and APT (Adaptive Proportion Test) Continuous Health Test (CHT) thresholds (see Section 4.4, SP800-90B). But you need the RNG to exist in order to set these thresholds and choose $H_{submitter}$ in order to calculate the assessed entropy. It's a chicken and egg scenario.

An option to resolve this dilemma is to design the RNG with flexible extractor ratio and flexible entropy thresholds on the RCT and APT tests so that they can be set after the entropy is assessed.

You want to set the CHT entropy thresholds to a value that will lead to data with entropy greater than or equal to $H_{submitter}$ will always pass the CHTs, while data from a broken noise source will always fail the CHTs. You want to set $H_{submitter}$ to be greater than the CHT thresholds and less than or equal to $\min(H_{original}, H_r, H_c)$.

An important insight here is that a real physical noise source will produce a distribution of entropy levels across time, environmental variation, and multiple devices. The SP800-90B procedures estimate a lower bound for the entropy for a sample of data from one device, at one point in time, and so the distribution is not comprehended or measured by the SP800-90B procedures. Setting $H_{submitter}$ to be below the lowest expected entropy from the distribution of entropy levels across devices is a method to get a consistent assessed entropy despite unreliable testing.

## 8.8  Collecting Noise Source Data

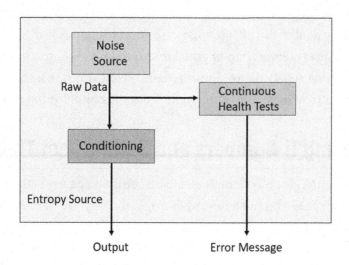

***Figure 8-4.***  *Entropy Source Model*

Figure 8-4 (based on Figure 1 from SP800-90B Section 2.2) describes the major logical blocks of an Entropy Source Model as defined by NIST. The SP800-90B standard specifies that data collected for entropy source assessment must be collected as "raw data" from the noise source before any manipulation (i.e., conditioning) of the data is performed.

The standard also specifies the data collected consist of samples of 1,000,000 contiguous symbols, so typically 1,000,000 bits or 1,000,000 bytes. Even though NIST does not require temperature or voltage sweeping for raw entropy collection used for entropy certification, claims for the performance of the noise source usually include an operating temperature range and, if the voltage can be varied, the operating voltage range. Noise source data samples should be collected at points within the operating voltage and temperature envelope.

For example, raw entropy data might be collected at 5°C intervals from a Tmin of –10°C to Tmax of 70°C plus an additional 5°C above Tmax and below Tmin. NIST does not specify the granularity required. The entropy data files would be collected from the raw data output, and the entropy report would list the filenames. The djent random data analysis software program accepts the encoding of voltage, temperature, chip ID, and process information in the filename, bracketed with underscores which can be seen in the following example, enabling these values to be included in the test output CSV. The voltage is fixed at 1V, due to a fixed voltage in the design, and the temperature is varied from –10°C to 110°C. Each file is 1MiByte in size, and the data is encoded in little-endian binary format. 1MiByte for each file is chosen because the largest symbol size for analysis by the SP800-90B entropy assessment (EA) tools is 1 million symbols. So, 1MiByte is sufficient for both analysis at 1 bit per symbol and 8 bits per symbol.

```
rawdata_CID-X1234_PROC-10nm_1p0V_-10p0C.bin
rawdata_CID-X1234_PROC-10nm_1p0V_-5p0C.bin
rawdata_CID-X1234_PROC-10nm_1p0V_0p0C.bin
rawdata_CID-X1234_PROC-10nm_1p0V_5p0C.bin
rawdata_CID-X1234_PROC-10nm_1p0V_10p0C.bin
rawdata_CID-X1234_PROC-10nm_1p0V_15p0C.bin
rawdata_CID-X1234_PROC-10nm_1p0V_20p0C.bin
rawdata_CID-X1234_PROC-10nm_1p0V_25p0C.bin
rawdata_CID-X1234_PROC-10nm_1p0V_30p0C.bin
rawdata_CID-X1234_PROC-10nm_1p0V_35p0C.bin
rawdata_CID-X1234_PROC-10nm_1p0V_40p0C.bin
rawdata_CID-X1234_PROC-10nm_1p0V_45p0C.bin
rawdata_CID-X1234_PROC-10nm_1p0V_50p0C.bin
rawdata_CID-X1234_PROC-10nm_1p0V_55p0C.bin
rawdata_CID-X1234_PROC-10nm_1p0V_60p0C.bin
rawdata_CID-X1234_PROC-10nm_1p0V_65p0C.bin
rawdata_CID-X1234_PROC-10nm_1p0V_70p0C.bin
rawdata_CID-X1234_PROC-10nm_1p0V_75p0C.bin
rawdata_CID-X1234_PROC-10nm_1p0V_80p0C.bin
rawdata_CID-X1234_PROC-10nm_1p0V_85p0C.bin
rawdata_CID-X1234_PROC-10nm_1p0V_90p0C.bin
rawdata_CID-X1234_PROC-10nm_1p0V_95p0C.bin
rawdata_CID-X1234_PROC-10nm_1p0V_100p0C.bin
rawdata_CID-X1234_PROC-10nm_1p0V_105p0C.bin
rawdata_CID-X1234_PROC-10nm_1p0V_110p0C.bin
```

Restart data must also be collected. This is a set of 1000 files, each of 1000 symbols. The data collected must be the first data to emit from the noise source after it is restarted, which might involve power cycling the noise source or resetting or otherwise getting it into its initial preoperational state. You should be able to argue why your choice of restart mechanism really does represent a full restart of the noise source. A file list might look as follows:

```
restartdata_CID-X1234_PROC-10nm_1p0V_25p0C_0.bin
restartdata_CID-X1234_PROC-10nm_1p0V_25p0C_1.bin
restartdata_CID-X1234_PROC-10nm_1p0V_25p0C_2.bin
...
restartdata_CID-X1234_PROC-10nm_1p0V_25p0C_997.bin
restartdata_CID-X1234_PROC-10nm_1p0V_25p0C_998.bin
restartdata_CID-X1234_PROC-10nm_1p0V_25p0C_999.bin
```

The restart data can be collected at normal operating conditions. It doesn't need to be collected across temperature or voltage.

The raw data entropy collection mechanism will depend on the specifics of the hardware design and so is out of scope for this book. Typically, there will be some configuration to put the RNG into a bypass mode, so the noise source data is available. A thermal head will be attached to the chip in question, or if it is a discrete board design, the board would be within a thermal chamber. Any chip or electronic product design lab would have these things available.

## 8.9  File Formats for Noise Source Data

The entropy assessment (EA) programs provided by NIST require data to be in a specific format where each symbol is encoded in a byte.

For example, if you were claiming to have a single-bit noise source (i.e., a noise source that generates one bit at a time), the bitstring 00101011 would be encoded in binary but as one bit per byte. That is, only bit 0 in each formatted byte would have real data, while bits 1–7 are padded with 0s. In other words, bitstring 00101011 would translate to

```
00000000
00000000
00000001
00000000
00000001
00000000
00000001
00000001
```

which is the same in hex as

0x00

0x00

0x01

0x00

0x01

0x00

0x01

0x01

Similarly, if you were to have a 4-bit per symbol noise source, the 00101011 bitstring would be encoded in binary bytes as 0x02 0x0B. That is, only bits 0–3 for each formatted byte would have real data, while bits 5–7 would be padded with 0s. In other words, bitstring 00101011 would translate to

00000010

00001011

which is the same in hex as

0x02

0x0B

And finally, if the source were an 8-bit per symbol noise source, 00101011 would be a normal 8-bit per formatted byte encoding 0x2B.

This means once you have collected the data, you need to reformat it into this strange format based on the symbol width you tell the software to use. The authors of this book refer to format as the "NIST Oddball" format. Note: This file format prevents you from representing symbols larger than 8 bits, since each symbol must fit in 1 byte.

# 8.10  Skipping Initial Data

SP800-90B requires an RNG to skip the initial data from a noise source to avoid potential low entropy output as the noise source starts up. This skipped data may be used later following a successful startup of the entropy source. For the raw data collection, you can also skip the initial data at the start of the data file while still having 1,000,000 symbols remaining, which means you will need to collect more than 1,000,000 bytes per file.

For restart data, you need 1000 symbols, so you may want to collect more than 1KiByte per file to again enable skipping the initial part of the file.

# 8.11  Software Tools for Processing Noise Source Data

In this section, we will look at some programs that can be used to format and test random data.

## 8.11.1  hexbinhex

hexbinhex is a set of programs to convert between binary, hexadecimal, ASCII binary (ASCII 1s and 0s), and the one-symbol-per-byte format used by the NIST programs.

The programs are hex2bin, bin2hex, bin2nistoddball, nistoddball2bin, bin201, and 012bin.

The code is in C and is available at https://github.com/dj-on-github/hexbinhex.

To get the code, clone it into a Unix-like environment such as Linux:

```
$ git clone https://github.com/dj-on-github/hexbinhex
Cloning into 'hexbinhex'...
remote: Enumerating objects: 79, done.
remote: Counting objects: 100% (8/8), done.
remote: Compressing objects: 100% (6/6), done.
remote: Total 79 (delta 2), reused 4 (delta 2), pack-reused 71
Receiving objects: 100% (79/79), 66.82 KiB | 3.18 MiB/s, done.
Resolving deltas: 100% (43/43), done.
```

Navigate into the hexbinhex directory:

```
$ cd hexbinhex
```

Build the code using make:

```
$ make
gcc -I/usr/local/include -m64 -g -Wall -L/usr/local/lib  hex2bin.c
-o hex2bin -lm
gcc -I/usr/local/include -m64 -g -Wall -L/usr/local/lib  bin2hex.c
-o bin2hex -lm
```

```
gcc -I/usr/local/include -m64 -g -Wall -L/usr/local/lib  bin2O1.c
-o bin2O1 -lm
gcc -I/usr/local/include -m64 -g -Wall -L/usr/local/lib
bin2nistoddball.c  -o bin2nistoddball -lm
gcc -I/usr/local/include -m64 -g -Wall -L/usr/local/lib
nistoddball2bin.c  -o nistoddball2bin -lm
```

Install the code with make install:

```
$ make install
cp bin2hex /usr/local/bin
cp bin2O1  /usr/local/bin
cp O12bin  /usr/local/bin
cp hex2bin /usr/local/bin
cp bin2nistoddball /usr/local/bin
cp nistoddball2bin /usr/local/bin
```

## 8.11.2  hex2bin

hex2bin does as the name suggests and converts ASCII hexadecimal files to binary.
There are other tools to do this, but it was added for completeness.

```
$ hex2bin -h
Usage: hex2bin [-h][-s lines_to_skip][-o <out filename>][filename]
     -s n           Skip the first n lines of the input text
     -o filename    Output to file filename instead of stdout
```

Convert hexadecimal data to binary.

## 8.11.3  bin2hex

bin2hex converts binary files to hexadecimal. The principal feature of this compared to
other converters is that it does not add any extra characters, like 0x prefixes or spaces
between groups of hex bytes. The width parameter gives the number of hex bytes (so 2
character pairs) per line with the default being 32.

```
$ bin2hex -h
Usage: bin2hex [-w <width>][-h][-o <out filename>] [filename]
```

Convert binary data to hexadecimal.

## 8.11.4  bin2nistoddball

bin2nistoddball converts binary data to the one-symbol-per-byte format used by the NIST tools. The program refers to the NIST format at the nistoddball format, since it is a very odd format. The –l parameter takes the symbol size between 1 and 8. It defaults to treating input data as little-endian bit order, but that can be reversed with -r. The output to the nistoddball format file defaults to little endian to match the input, but that can be reversed with -B. The authors use the .nob file extension name for the nistoddball format files.

### $ **bin2nistoddball -h**

```
Usage: bin2nistoddball [-l <bits_per_symbol 1-8>][-B|-L][-v][-h][-o <out
filename>] [filename]
        -l , --length <bits_per_symbol 1-8> Set the number of bits to encode
                in each output byte
        -r , --reverse                  Interpret input binary data as
                                        big endian (MSB first) (default
                                        is little endian)
        -B , --bigendian                Unpack output multi-bit symbols
                                        as big-endian (msb first)
        -L , --littleendian             Unpack output multi-bit symbols
                                        as little-endian (lsb first)
                                        (default)
        -v , --verbose                  Output information to stderr
        -h , --help                     Output this information
```

Convert binary data to NIST Oddball SP800-90B one-symbol-per-byte format.

## 8.11.5  nistoddball2bin

nistoddball2bin does the reverse of bin2nistoddball:

### $ **nistoddball2bin -h**

```
Usage: nistoddball2bin [-l <bits_per_symbol 1-8>][-B|-L][-v][-h][-o <out
filename>] [filename]
        -l n            Set the number of symbol bits per byte encoded in the
                        input data. Must be between 1 to 8
```

| -B | Interpret the input symbols at being big endian (MSB first) |
| -L | Interpret the input symbols at being little endian (LSB first) (default) |
| -v | Verbose mode. Outputs information to stderr |
| -h | Display this information |
| -o filename | Output to file filename instead of stdout |

Convert binary data to NIST Oddball SP800-90B one-symbol-per-byte format.

Notes:

The NIST format for SP800-90B testing requires symbols to be as one symbol per bit.

This means only symbols of sizes 1 through 8 bits can be supported.

The bit ordering of the bits within the symbols is not specified by NIST. The -L and -B options allow you to choose.

The output binary data by default is in little endian format, with the lower order bits in bytes coming before higher order bits. This can be reversed with the -r option.

bin201 and 012bin are included but not relevant to the file formats used in entropy collection and analysis. Thus, the details are left out from this book. They convert between binary bytes, for example, 0x5A, and ASCII representation with 0s and 1s, for example, "01011010".

# 8.11.6 Restart_slicer

restart_slicer takes 1000 files of restart data and converts it to a NIST matrix file format for use by ea_restart. Each file must contain 1000 or more symbols. Only the first 1000 symbols from each file will be used, unless the options to skip initial data are invoked, where a 1000-symbol substring will be used from the position you specify.

The code can be cloned from GitHub at https://github.com/dj-on-github/restart_test_sp800-90b.

**$ restart_slicer -h**
Usage: restart_slicer [-l <bits_per_symbol 1-8>][-B|-L][-v][-h][-o <out filename>] [filename_glob_pattern]

```
-l , --length <bits_per_symbol 1-8> Set the number of bits to encode
        in eat output byte
-s , --skip <bits_per_symbol 1-8> Number of bytes to skip in each
        binary file
-r , --reverse                       Interpret input binary data as
                                     big endian (MSB first) (default
                                     is little endian)
-B , --bigendian                     Unpack output multi-bit symbols
                                     as big-endian (msb first)
-L , --littleendian                  Unpack output multi-bit symbols
                                     as little-endian (lsb first)
                                     (default)
-v , --verbose                       Output information to stderr
-h , --help                          Output this information
```

Convert 1000 binary data files to NIST Oddball restart format in SP800-90B one-symbol-per-byte format.

The filename glob pattern is used to specify the 1000 files. It must be enclosed in quotes in order to prevent the shell expanding the glob pattern before sending it to restart_slicer.

For the purposes of this example, a program to make a command file to make 1000 test files in a subdirectory was written in python and run:

```
#!/usr/bin/env python3

for i in range(1000):
    command = "djenrandom -b -s -m markov_2_param --bias=0.4
    --correlation=-0.1 -k 1 -o restart_data_%d.bin" % i
    print(command)
```

We run the python to make the command file and run the command file to make the data files:

```
$ python3 make_testcommands.py > make_testfiles.sh
$ sh make_testfiles.sh
```

This gives us 1000 files with 1KiByte of data each and with a bias of 0.4 and serial correlation of –0.1.

restart_data_0.nob
restart_data_1.nob
restart_data_2.nob
...
restart_data_998.nob
restart_data_999.nob

With the test data, we can now run `restart_slicer` over it. The result matrix file will be used with ea_restart described in the next section. The `-l 1` parameter tells `restart_slicer` to encode the data as 1 bit per symbol:

```
$ restart_slicer -l 1 -o matrix.nob 'test_data/restart_data_*.bin'
Wrote restart file matrix.nob to disk.
```

## 8.11.7  NIST ea_non_iid, ea_iid, restart

NIST provides a suite of entropy assessment (EA) programs that implement to testing in SP800-90B.

This can be found on GitHub at https://github.com/usnistgov/SP800-90B_EntropyAssessment.

To download the code with git:

```
$ git clone https://github.com/usnistgov/SP800-90B_EntropyAssessment
Cloning into 'SP800-90B_EntropyAssessment'...
remote: Enumerating objects: 2214, done.
remote: Counting objects: 100% (344/344), done.
remote: Compressing objects: 100% (93/93), done.
remote: Total 2214 (delta 278), reused 253 (delta 251), pack-reused 1870
Receiving objects: 100% (2214/2214), 11.98 MiB | 12.64 MiB/s, done.
Resolving deltas: 100% (1452/1452), done.
```

To compile, you must descend into the cpp subdirectory of the SP800-90B_EntropyAssessment directory and type make:

```
$ cd SP800-90B_EntropyAssessment/cpp
```

On Ubuntu Linux 20.04.1 LTS, we are given instructions to install several dependencies and then type make:

```
$ sudo apt-get install libbz2-dev libdivsufsort-dev libjsoncpp-dev libssl-
dev libmpfr-dev
Reading package lists... Done
Building dependency tree
Reading state information... Done
libbz2-dev is already the newest version (1.0.8-2).
libjsoncpp-dev is already the newest version (1.7.4-3.1ubuntu2).
libmpfr-dev is already the newest version (4.0.2-1).
libssl-dev is already the newest version (1.1.1f-1ubuntu2.13).
The following package was automatically installed and is no longer
required:
  libfprint-2-tod1
Use 'sudo apt autoremove' to remove it.
The following additional packages will be installed:
  libdivsufsort3
The following NEW packages will be installed:
  libdivsufsort-dev libdivsufsort3
0 upgraded, 2 newly installed, 0 to remove and 209 not upgraded.
Need to get 61.8 kB of archives.
After this operation, 172 kB of additional disk space will be used.
Do you want to continue? [Y/n] Y
Get:1 http://us.archive.ubuntu.com/ubuntu focal/universe amd64
libdivsufsort3 amd64 2.0.1-4 [42.4 kB]
Get:2 http://us.archive.ubuntu.com/ubuntu focal/universe amd64
libdivsufsort-dev amd64 2.0.1-4 [19.4 kB]
Fetched 61.8 kB in 0s (178 kB/s)
Selecting previously unselected package libdivsufsort3:amd64.
(Reading database ... 263125 files and directories currently installed.)
Preparing to unpack .../libdivsufsort3_2.0.1-4_amd64.deb ...
Unpacking libdivsufsort3:amd64 (2.0.1-4) ...
Selecting previously unselected package libdivsufsort-dev:amd64.
Preparing to unpack .../libdivsufsort-dev_2.0.1-4_amd64.deb ...
```

```
Unpacking libdivsufsort-dev:amd64 (2.0.1-4) ...
Setting up libdivsufsort3:amd64 (2.0.1-4) ...
Setting up libdivsufsort-dev:amd64 (2.0.1-4) ...
Processing triggers for libc-bin (2.31-0ubuntu9.7) ...
```

$ **make**
```
g++ -std=c++11 -fopenmp -O2 -ffloat-store -I/usr/include/jsoncpp
-msse2 -march=native  iid_main.cpp -o ea_iid -lbz2 -lpthread
-ldivsufsort  -ljsoncpp -lssl -lcrypto
g++ -std=c++11 -fopenmp -O2 -ffloat-store -I/usr/include/jsoncpp
-msse2 -march=native  non_iid_main.cpp -o ea_non_iid -lbz2 -lpthread
-ldivsufsort  -ljsoncpp -lssl -lcrypto
g++ -std=c++11 -fopenmp -O2 -ffloat-store -I/usr/include/jsoncpp
-msse2 -march=native  restart_main.cpp -o ea_restart -lbz2 -lpthread
-ldivsufsort  -ljsoncpp -lssl -lcrypto
g++ -std=c++11 -fopenmp -O2 -ffloat-store -I/usr/include/jsoncpp -msse2
-march=native  conditioning_main.cpp -o ea_conditioning -lbz2 -lpthread
-ldivsufsort  -lmpfr -lgmp -ljsoncpp -lssl -lcrypto
g++ -std=c++11 -fopenmp -O2 -ffloat-store -I/usr/include/jsoncpp -msse2
-march=native  transpose_main.cpp -o ea_transpose -lbz2 -lpthread
-ldivsufsort  -ljsoncpp -lssl -lcrypto
```

This yields five executables:

$ **ls ea_* | cat**
```
ea_conditioning
ea_iid
ea_non_iid
ea_restart
ea_transpose
```

The makefile delivered with the NIST code does not provide an install option, so it must be done manually. The executables can be copied to /usr/local/bin, so they are available from the command line:

$ **sudo cp ea_* /usr/local/bin**

# 8.11.8 ea_conditioning

ea_conditioning computes the output entropy for vetted and non-vetted conditioning components:

**$ ea_conditioning**
Incorrect usage.
Usage is: ea_conditioning -v [-q] <n_in> <n_out> <nw> <h_in> [-o filename.json]

> or
>
> ea_conditioning -n <n_in> <n_out> <nw> <h_in> [h' | -i filename]
> [-o filename.json]

> <n_in>: input number of bits to conditioning function.
> <n_out>: output number of bits from conditioning function.
> <nw>: narrowest internal width of conditioning function.
> <h_in>: input entropy to conditioning function.
> <-v|-n>: '-v' for vetted conditioning function, '-n' for non-vetted conditioning function. Vetted conditioning is the default.
> <h'>: entropy estimate per bit of conditioned sequential dataset (only for '-n' option).
> -q: Quiet mode, less output to screen.
> -i: Input file name, to run an entropy assessment on a non-vetted conditioned data file and use that value as h'.

> This program computes the entropy of the output of a conditioning function 'h_out' (Section 3.1.5).
> If the conditioning function is vetted, then

> > h_out = Output_Entropy(n_in, n_out, nw, h_in)

> where 'Output_Entropy' is specified in Section 3.1.5.1.2. If the conditioning function is non-vetted then

> > h_out = min(Output_Entropy(n_in, n_out, nw, h_in), 0.999*n_out, h'*n_out)

> as stated in Section 3.1.5.2.

-o: Set Output Type to JSON

    Changes the output format to JSON and sets the file location
    for the output file.

--version: Prints tool version information

A vetted conditioning component is evaluated using four parameters:

- n_in: The number of bits of input data. Typically, a multiple of the input block size of the conditioning algorithm.

- n_out: The number of bits of output data. This must be less than n_in and is typically equal to the block size of the output of the cryptographic function or the size of the output after truncation is applied.

- nw: The internal width of the cryptographic function used in the conditioner. The widths are given in Table 1 of SP800-90B. This has been reproduced in Figure 8-5.

- h_in: The number of bits of entropy in the n_in input bits. This is equal to the entropy rate multiplied by the assessed entropy.

| Table 1 The narrowest internal width and output lengths of the vetted conditioning functions. | | |
|---|---|---|
| **Conditioning Function** | **Narrowest Internal Width** $(nw)$ | **Output Length** $(n_{out})$ |
| HMAC | hash-function output size | hash-function output size |
| CMAC | AES block size = 128 | AES block size = 128 |
| CBC-MAC | AES block size = 128 | AES block size = 128 |
| Hash Function | hash-function output size | hash-function output size |
| Hash_df | hash-function output size | hash-function output size |
| Block_Cipher_df | AES key size | AES key size |

***Figure 8-5.*** *Image of Table 1 from SP800-90B, Giving Conditioner Algorithm Internal Widths*

As an example, for a vetted conditioner with a 6:1 ratio of n_in to n_out, an assessed entropy rate of 0.5, and using CBC-MAC, the ea_conditioning function could be invoked as follows, with 768 for n_in, 128 for n_out, 128 for nw, and 384 for h_in computed at 0.5*768:

```
$ ea_conditioning -v 768 128 128 384 -o conditioner.json
n_in = 768
n_out = 128
nw = 128
h_in = 384
Attempting to compute entropy with 1536 bits of precision.
Output_Entropy(*) = 128; Close to n_out (epsilon =
2^(-262.4712336270551023831)); Close to nw (epsilon =
2^(-262.4712336270551023831))
(Vetted) h_out = 128
epsilon = 2^(-262.4712336270551023831): SP 800-90B 2012 Draft and SP
800-90C 2021 Draft Full Entropy
```

The output is also encoded in the output JSON file. Hang on to this file. You may need to submit it with the other documentation or at least include the test in the entropy justification report.

You can see how the SHA256 algorithm has been assumed, which is incorrect as we put in 128 to reflect the nw and n_out of AES-CBC-MAC. This does not affect the result though.

```
$ cat conditioner.json
{
   "IID" : false,
   "dateTimeStamp" : "20220507174504",
   "errorLevel" : 0,
   "filename" : "",
   "sha256" : "",
   "testCases" : [
      {
         "h_in" : 100,
         "h_out" : 99.99999999462554,
         "n_in" : 768,
```

```
        "n_out" : 128,
        "nw" : 128,
        "testCaseDesc" : "Overall"
     }
  ],
  "toolVersion" : "1.1.3",
  "type" : "Conditioning"
}
```

To interpret these results, you are looking for epsilon to be less than $2^{-32}$ in the preceding ea_conditioning example. Search for the text "SP 800-90B 2012 Draft and SP800-90C 2021 Draft Full Entropy" in its output. This bound is set in the SP800-90C, which at the time of writing is still a draft standard. It is good practice to exceed this value (i.e., have an epsilon $< 2^{-32}$), as the example result has, with $2^{-262}$ being much smaller than $2^{-32}$. To protect against changes in the standard, we would recommend achieving epsilon $< 2^{-64}$. There have been some calls for the bound in the SP800-90C draft to be reduced while the document is still subject to comment and revision.

It is also worth running this multiple times, while varying h_in, to find the lowest entropy rate that would yield epsilon $< 2^{-32}$. This will give you the lower bound input requirement for the conditioner.

Common values for the vetted conditioners are shown as follows; the efficiency value is the ratio of entropy out to entropy in, or n_out/h_in at the minimum entropy rate entered. For each n_in, a binary chop was done on the entropy rate to find the smallest entropy rate that would yield full entropy output:

```
AES-CBC-MAC Extraction, n_out = 128
n_in=    256.0  effcy=0.7973   min_input_entropy_rate= 0.6271
n_in=    384.0  effcy=0.7973   min_input_entropy_rate= 0.4181
n_in=    512.0  effcy=0.7972   min_input_entropy_rate= 0.3136
n_in=    640.0  effcy=0.7971   min_input_entropy_rate= 0.2509
n_in=    768.0  effcy=0.7971   min_input_entropy_rate= 0.2091
n_in=    896.0  effcy=0.7972   min_input_entropy_rate= 0.1792
HMAC/SHA-256 Extraction, n_out = 256
n_in=    384.0  effcy=0.8872   min_input_entropy_rate= 0.7514
n_in=    512.0  effcy=0.8872   min_input_entropy_rate= 0.5636
```

```
n_in=     640.0  effcy=0.8871   min_input_entropy_rate= 0.4509
n_in=     768.0  effcy=0.8872   min_input_entropy_rate= 0.3757
n_in=     896.0  effcy=0.8870   min_input_entropy_rate= 0.3221
HMAC/SHA-384 Extraction, n_out = 256
n_in=     384.0  effcy=0.8872   min_input_entropy_rate= 0.7514
n_in=     512.0  effcy=0.8872   min_input_entropy_rate= 0.5636
n_in=     640.0  effcy=0.8871   min_input_entropy_rate= 0.4509
n_in=     768.0  effcy=0.8872   min_input_entropy_rate= 0.3757
n_in=     896.0  effcy=0.8870   min_input_entropy_rate= 0.3221
HMAC/SHA-512 Extraction, n_out = 256
n_in=     384.0  effcy=0.8872   min_input_entropy_rate= 0.7514
n_in=     512.0  effcy=0.8872   min_input_entropy_rate= 0.5636
n_in=     640.0  effcy=0.8871   min_input_entropy_rate= 0.4509
n_in=     768.0  effcy=0.8872   min_input_entropy_rate= 0.3757
n_in=     896.0  effcy=0.8870   min_input_entropy_rate= 0.3221
HMAC/SHA-512 Extraction, n_out = 256
n_in=     384.0  effcy=0.8872   min_input_entropy_rate= 0.7514
n_in=     512.0  effcy=0.8872   min_input_entropy_rate= 0.5636
n_in=     640.0  effcy=0.8871   min_input_entropy_rate= 0.4509
n_in=     768.0  effcy=0.8872   min_input_entropy_rate= 0.3757
n_in=     896.0  effcy=0.8870   min_input_entropy_rate= 0.3221
```

The -n option for a non-vetted conditioner gives a result that will not achieve full entropy regardless of the conditioner design. This means that in a compliant RNG, the last conditioner in a chain of conditioners must be a vetted one. The usual configuration is just a single vetted conditioner, but that may be preceded with vetted or non-vetted conditioners. It also uses the assessed entropy rate of the input. Here, we will assume it to be 0.95 as the assessed entropy rate of the full entropy output from a non-vetted conditioner, which is consistent with what ea_non_iid would return over full entropy data. Here, we see the same parameters as the previous example, but with the -n option added. The result gives (non-vetted) h_out = 121.599... instead of (Vetted) h_out = 128:

```
$ ea_conditioning -n 768 128 128 384 0.95 -o conditioner.json
n_in = 768
n_out = 128
```

nw = 128
h_in = 384
h' = 0.9499999999999999999891
Attempting to compute entropy with 1536 bits of precision.
Output_Entropy(*) = 128; Close to n_out (epsilon =
2^(-262.4712336270551023831)); Close to nw (epsilon =
2^(-262.4712336270551023831))
0.999 * n_out = 127.8719999999999999973
h' * n_out = 121.5999999999999999986
**(Non-vetted) h_out = 121.5999999999999999986**

## 8.11.9  ea_iid

ea_iid computes the entropy of data assumed to be IID, following the IID track
procedures:

$ **ea_iid**
Incorrect usage.
Usage is: ea_iid [-i|-c] [-a|-t] [-v] [-q] [-l <index>,<samples> ] <file_
name> [bits_per_symbol]

> <file_name>: Must be relative path to a binary file with at least 1
> million entries (samples).
> [bits_per_symbol]: Must be between 1-8, inclusive. By default this
> value is inferred from the data.
> [-i|-c]: '-i' for initial entropy estimate, '-c' for conditioned
> sequential dataset entropy estimate. The initial entropy estimate is
> the default.
> [-a|-t]: '-a' produces the 'H_bitstring' assessment using all read
> bits, '-t' truncates the bitstring used to produce the `H_bitstring`
> assessment to 1000000 bits. Test all data by default.
> Note: When testing binary data, no `H_bitstring` assessment is
> produced, so the `-a` and `-t` options produce the same results for
> the initial assessment of binary data.
> -v: Optional verbosity flag for more output. Can be used
> multiple times.

-q: Quiet mode, less output to screen. This will override any verbose flags.

-l <index>,<samples>        Read the <index> substring of length <samples>.

Samples are assumed to be packed into 8-bit values, where the least significant 'bits_per_symbol'
bits constitute the symbol.

-i: Initial Entropy Estimate (Section 3.1.3)

> Computes the initial entropy estimate H_I as described in Section 3.1.3
> (not accounting for H_submitter) using the entropy estimators specified in
> Section 6.3.  If 'bits_per_symbol' is greater than 1, the samples are also
> converted to bitstrings and assessed to create H_bitstring; for multi-bit symbols,
> two entropy estimates are computed: H_original and H_bitstring.
> Returns min(H_original, bits_per_symbol X H_bitstring). The initial entropy
> estimate H_I = min(H_submitter, H_original, bits_per_symbol X H_bitstring).

-c: Conditioned Sequential Dataset Entropy Estimate (Section 3.1.5.2)

> Computes the entropy estimate per bit h' for the conditioned sequential dataset if the
> conditioning function is non-vetted. The samples are converted to a bitstring.
> Returns h' = min(H_bitstring).

-o: Set Output Type to JSON

> Changes the output format to JSON and sets the file location for the output file.

--version: Prints tool version information

To run ea_iid, we need some sample data. The standard requires the input data to be 1,000,000 symbols long. We can generate 1,000,000 IID samples using djenrandom. It is given a bias of 0.6 and a resulting entropy rate of 0.737:

```
$ djenrandom -b -m biased --bias=0.6 -k 128 -o biased0p6.bin
```

We convert this to the nistoddball format with 1-bit symbols:

```
$ bin2nistoddball -l 1 biased0p6.bin > biased0p6.nob
```

Then we can attempt to run it through ea_iid. We expect a result below 0.737, but it should be close. Any significant difference with 0.737 min-entropy rate represents a failure of the test. A worse failure would be the program crashing, which is exactly what it does:

```
$ ea_iid -i -t -l 0,1000000 -o iid_result.json biased0p6.nob 1
Segmentation fault (core dumped)
```

Removing the -l 0,1000000 option, which tells it to use the first 1,000,000 symbols appears to be a workaround for the bug. This may be fixed by the time you download the code:

```
$ ea_iid -i -t -o iid_result.json biased0p6.nob 1
Calculating baseline statistics...
H_original: 0.735506
** Passed chi square tests

** Passed length of longest repeated substring test

** Passed IID permutation tests
```

From this, we get $H_{original}$ which is used in the claims that are made in the entropy report.

# 8.11.10  ea_non_iid

ea_non_iid computes the entropy of data assumed to be non-IID, following the non-IID track procedures. This will generally be the track you use since making and proving an IID claim is very difficult and offers little benefit since you will still need a conditioner:

## $ **ea_non_iid**

Incorrect usage.

Usage is: ea_non_iid [-i|-c] [-a|-t] [-v] [-q] [-l <index>,<samples> ] <file_name> [bits_per_symbol]

<file_name>: Must be relative path to a binary file with at least 1 million entries (samples).

[bits_per_symbol]: Must be between 1-8, inclusive. By default this value is inferred from the data.

[-i|-c]: '-i' for initial entropy estimate, '-c' for conditioned sequential dataset entropy estimate. The initial entropy estimate is the default.

[-a|-t]: '-a' produces the 'H_bitstring' assessment using all read bits, '-t' truncates the bitstring used to produce the `H_bitstring` assessment to 1000000 bits. Test all data by default.

Note: When testing binary data, no `H_bitstring` assessment is produced, so the `-a` and `-t` options produce the same results for the initial assessment of binary data.

-v: Optional verbosity flag for more output. Can be used multiple times.

-q: Quiet mode, less output to screen. This will override any verbose flags.

-l <index>,<samples>        Read the <index> substring of length <samples>.

Samples are assumed to be packed into 8-bit values, where the least significant 'bits_per_symbol'
bits constitute the symbol.

-i: Initial Entropy Estimate (Section 3.1.3)

Computes the initial entropy estimate H_I as described in Section 3.1.3
(not accounting for H_submitter) using the entropy estimators specified in
Section 6.3.  If 'bits_per_symbol' is greater than 1, the samples are also

converted to bitstrings and assessed to create H_bitstring; for multi-bit symbols,
two entropy estimates are computed: H_original and H_bitstring.
Returns min(H_original, bits_per_symbol X H_bitstring). The initial entropy
estimate H_I = min(H_submitter, H_original, bits_per_symbol X H_bitstring).

-c: Conditioned Sequential Dataset Entropy Estimate (Section 3.1.5.2)

Computes the entropy estimate per bit h' for the conditioned sequential dataset if the
conditioning function is non-vetted. The samples are converted to a bitstring.
Returns h' = min(H_bitstring).

-o: Set Output Type to JSON

Changes the output format to JSON and sets the file location for the output file.

--version: Prints tool version information

To run ea_non_iid, we need some sample data. The standard requires the input data to be 1,000,000 symbols long. We can generate 1,000,000 IID samples using djenrandom. It is given a bias of 0.4 and serial correlation of –0.1 with a resulting entropy rate of 0.644:

```
$ djenrandom -b -m markov_2_param --bias=0.4 --correlation=-0.1 -k 128 -o
bias0p4scc-0p1.bin
```

We convert this to the nistoddball format with 1-bit symbols:

```
$ bin2nistoddball bias0p4scc-0p1.bin > bias0p4scc-0p1.nob
```

Then we can attempt to run it through ea_non_iid. We expect a result below 0.644, but it should be close. Any significant difference with 0.644 min-entropy rate represents a failure of the test.

The ea_non_iid program has the same bug as with ea_iid, where it crashes when passed the -l 0,1000000 option:

```
$ ea_non_iid -i -t -l 0,1000000 -o non_iid_result.json bias0p4scc-0p1-nob 1
Segmentation fault (core dumped)
```

Trying again without the -l option, we get

```
$ ea_non_iid -i -t -o non_iid_result.json bias0p4scc-0p1.nob 1
Running non-IID tests...

Running Most Common Value Estimate...

Running Entropic Statistic Estimates (bit strings only)...

Running Tuple Estimates...

Running Predictor Estimates...

H_original: 0.503877
```

From this, we get $H_{original}$ which is used in the claims that are made in the entropy justification report. In this case, we know the actual min-entropy of 0.644, mathematically derived from the model that generated the data. This represents a gross underestimate of the actual entropy. The size of the underestimation seems to be larger with data that has serial correlation, and you should plan accordingly to overprovision your entropy to account for the highly inaccurate SP800-90B non-IID tests. It is not worth waiting for NIST to fix their tests, since the defects have been around for many years. NIST has made no effort to fix them despite papers being published describing the mathematical flaws.

## 8.11.11  ea_restart

ea_restart analyzes the restart data and computes the assessed entropy as a minimum of its own analysis and the $H_{original}$ value that you supply based on the ea_non_iid or ea_iid testing:

```
$ ea_restart -h
ea_restart: invalid option -- 'h'
```

Usage is: ea_restart [-i|-n] [-v] [-q] <file_name> [bits_per_symbol] <H_I>

<file_name>: Must be relative path to a binary file with at least 1 million entries (samples),
and in the "row dataset" format described in SP800-90B Section 3.1.4.1.
[bits_per_symbol]: Must be between 1-8, inclusive.
<H_I>: Initial entropy estimate.
[-i|-n]: '-i' for IID data, '-n' for non-IID data. Non-IID is the default.
-v: Optional verbosity flag for more output.
-q: Quiet mode, less output to screen.

Restart samples are assumed to be packed into 8-bit values, where the rightmost 'bits_per_symbol'
bits constitute the sample.

This program performs restart testing as described in Restart Tests (Section 3.1.4). The data
consists of 1000 restarts, each with 1000 samples. The data is converted to rows and columns
as described Section 3.1.4.1. The sanity check (Section 3.1.4.3) and the validation test
(Section 3.1.4.2) are performed on this data.

If the restart data passes the sanity check and validation test, this program returns
min(H_r, H_c, H_I), which is either the validated entropy assessment or used to derive
'h_in' if conditioning is used (Section 3.1.5).

--version: Prints tool version information

The program is passed the matrix.nob file that was created with restart_slicer:

```
$ ea_restart -n matrix.nob 1 0.503877
H_I: 0.503877
ALPHA: 5.0251553006530614e-06, X_cutoff: 767
X_max: 648
```

Running non-IID tests...

Running Most Common Value Estimate...

Running Entropic Statistic Estimates (bit strings only)...

Running Tuple Estimates...

Running Predictor Estimates...

H_r: 0.507140
H_c: 0.523209
H_I: 0.503877

Validation Test Passed...

min(H_r, H_c, H_I): 0.503877

The final number given is the assessed entropy.

## 8.11.12  ea_transpose

ea_transpose takes a matrix file of the restart data, as produced by restart_slicer, and computes the transpose of the matrix. This transposed matrix file is used in the Section 5 tests for testing the IID assumption, along with the normal matrix file. Results in an IID claim should present the data from both analyses.

```
$ ea_transpose -h
ea_transpose: invalid option -- 'h'
Usage is: ea_transpose [-v] [-l <index>] <file> <outfile>
        [-v]: Increase verbosity.
        [-l <index>]      Read the <index> substring of 1000000 samples.
        <file>: File with (blocks of) 1000 sets of restart data, each set
        being 1000 samples.
        The result is saved in <file>.column
        This program computes the transpose of the restart matrix, and
        produces column data appropriate testing with the other tools.
        This helps to support the testing described in SP800-90B
        Section 3.1.2 #3

        --version: Prints tool version information
```

We make the transpose file by passing in the original row-oriented matrix file:

```
$ ea_transpose matrix.nob matrix_transpose.nob
$ ls matrix*
matrix.nob  matrix_transpose.nob
```

## 8.11.13 djent

djent performs a statistical analysis of noise source output data. It is a reimplementation of the much older program "ent" by John Walker. It is not specifically needed or called out in SP800-90B, but in making claims based on the analysis of the data in the entropy report, the statistics computed by djent or any similar program will be needed.

djent can be cloned from GitHub:

```
$ git clone https://github.com/dj-on-github/djent
Cloning into 'djent'...
remote: Enumerating objects: 280, done.
remote: Counting objects: 100% (13/13), done.
remote: Compressing objects: 100% (10/10), done.
remote: Total 280 (delta 5), reused 11 (delta 3), pack-reused 267
Receiving objects: 100% (280/280), 474.43 KiB | 15.30 MiB/s, done.
Resolving deltas: 100% (146/146), done.
```

It is built with make and installed with make install:

```
$ cd djent
$ make
gcc -c -I/usr/local/include -m64 -g -Wall -o djent.o djent.c
gcc -I/usr/local/include -m64 -g -Wall -L/usr/local/lib  djent.o -o djent
-lm -lgmp -lmpfr
$ sudo make install
$ cp djent /usr/local/bin
```

The help information is extensive:

```
$ djent -h
Usage: djent [-brRpcCuhds] [-l <n>] [-i <input file list filename>]
[filename] [filename2] ...
```

Compute statistics of random data.
  Author: David Johnston, dj@deadhat.com

| | | |
|---|---|---|
| -i \<filename\> | --inputfilelist=\<filename\> | Read list of filenames from \<filename\> |
| -p | --parse_filename | Extract CID, Process, Voltage and Temperature from filename. The values will be included in the output. |
| -l \<n\> | --symbol_length=\<n\> | Treat incoming data symbols as bitlength n. Default is 8. |
| -b | --binary | Treat incoming data as binary. Default bit length will be -l 1 |
| -r | --byte_reverse | Reverse the bit order in incoming bytes |
| -R | --word_reverse | Reverse the byte order in incoming 4 byte words |
| -c | --occurrence | Print symbol occurrence counts |
| -C | --longest | Print symbol longest run counts |
| -w | --scc_wrap | Treat data as cyclical in SCC |
| -n \<n\> | --lagn=\<n\> | Lag gap in SCC. Default=1 |
| -S \<n\> | --skip=\<n\> | Skip over \<n\> initial symbols |
| -L \<n\> | --substring=\<n\> | Analyse no more that \<n\> symbols |
| -f | --fold | Fold uppercase letters to lower case |
| -t | --terse | Terse output |
| -e | --ent_exact | Exactly match output format of ent |
| -s | --suppress_header | Suppress the header in terse output |
| -h or -u | --help | Print this text |

Notes
  * By default djent is in hex mode where it reads ascii hex data and
    converts it to binary to analyze.

In hex mode, the symbol length defaults to 8, so normal hex files can be treated as a representation
of bytes. The symbol length can be changed to any value between 1 and 32 bits using the -l <n> option.

* With the -b option djent switches to binary reads in each byte as binary with a symbol length of 1.
* To analyze ascii text instead of hex ascii, you need djent to treat each byte as a separate symbol, so
use binary mode with a symbol length of 8. I.E. djent -b -l 8 <filename>
* By default djent treats the MSB of each byte as the first. This can be switched so that djent treats
the LSB as the first bit in each byte using the -r option.
* Terse output is requested using -t. This outputs in CSV format. The first line is the header. If
multiple files are provided, there will be one line of CSV output per file in addition to the header.
The CSV header can be suppressed with -s.
* To analyze multiple files, just give multiple file names on the command line. To read data in from
the command line, don't provide a filename and pipe the data in.
<datasource> | djent
* The parse filename option =p picks takes four patterns from the filename to include in the output,
This is so that it is easy to plot test conditions that are commonly encoded in a filename.
Fields are delimited by uderscores. The four patters for CID, process, Voltage and Temperature are:
_CID-<componentID>_ , _PROC-<process info>_, _<x>p<y>V_ and _<x>p<y>C_
. 'p' is the decimal point.
* To compute the statistics, djent builds a frequency table of the symbols. This can be displayed
using the -c option. The size of this table is what limits the the maximum symbol size. For each

of the 2^n symbols, a 64 bit entry in a table is created. So for n=32, that's 32GBytes so the ability
to handle large symbol sizes is limited by the available memory and the per process allocation limit.

* The serial correlation coefficient is not wrap around by default, meaning that it does not compare
the last value in the data with the first. To get wrap around behaviour, use the -w option.

* The Lag-N correlation coefficient can be computed by using the -n <n> option. This causes the SCC

computation to compare each Xth symbol with the (X+n)th symbol instead of the (X+1)th symbol.
If you use wrap around with Lag-N, then the wrap around will reach n bits further into the start
of the sequence.

* The byte reverse option -r reverses the order of bits within each byte. The word reverse option -R
reverses the order of bytes within each 32 bit word, from 3,2,1,0 to 0,1,2,3. Both -R and -r can
be used together. Using -R with a data that isn't a multiple of 32 bits long will get padded with

zeros, which may not be what you want. A padding warning will be sent to STDERR.

* Instead of providing data file names on the command line, djent can be told to read a list of files
from a text file. The file must have one filename per line. Lines beginning with # will be ignored.
Use the -i <filename> option to request that djent reads the file list from <filename>.

Examples
  Print this help
    djent -h

  Analyze hex file from stdin
    cat datafile.hex | djent

Analyze binary file
  djent -b datafile.bin

Analyze several files with CSV output
  djent -t data1.hex data2.hex data3.hex

Analyze ascii symbols - Read in binary and set symbol size to 8.
  djent -b -l 8  textfile.txt

Analyze binary file with parsable filename.
  djent -b -t -p  rawdata_CID-X23_PROC-TTFT_1p2V_25p0C_.bin

There are many options with djent, but the command-line help information is much more detailed than for the NIST tools.

This is a simple example of analyzing the binary data with bias and serial correlation created earlier for the ea_non_iid test:

**$ djent -b -l 1 bias0p4scc-0.1.bin**
```
 opening bias0p4scc-0.1.bin as binary
 Symbol Size(bits) = 1
   Min Entropy (by max occurrence of symbol 0) = 0.738233
   Analysing 1048568 1-bit symbols
   Shannon IID Entropy = 0.971258 bits per symbol
   Optimal compression would compress by 2.874207 percent
   Chi square: symbol count=1048569, distribution=41502.00, randomly
   exceeds 0.00 percent of the time
   Mean = 0.400527
   Monte Carlo value for Pi is 3.708125 (error 18.03 percent).
   Serial Correlation = -0.101012
   Longest Run Symbol = 0. Run Length = 22
   Probabilty of longest run being <= 22 = 0.882498
   Position of Longest Run = 30846 (0x787e). Byte position 3855 (0xf0f)
```

For analyzing larger amounts of data, multiple files can be passed in on the command line. A file containing a list of files to be processed can be passed in with the -i <filename> option. The output can be put in CSV format with the -t (or --terse) option. The length of the symbols being processed is given with the -l <length in bits> option. In the preceding example, we see the min-entropy computed from the occurrence of the most common symbol 0. At 1 bit per symbol, this is not a valid measurement as described in Section 8.1. Doing the analysis with 8 bits per symbol brings the effects of the serial correlation into account, and so the min-entropy value is more accurate with enough data and long enough symbols, but for data characterized by bias and serial correlation, a Markov analysis can give an exact, analytic measurement, which is described in SP800-90B.

```
$ djent -b -l 8 bias0p4scc-0.1.bin
 opening bias0p4scc-0.1.bin as binary
 Symbol Size(bits) = 8
   Min Entropy (by max occurrence of symbol 0) = 0.822768
   Analysing 131071 8-bit symbols
   Shannon IID Entropy = 7.716623 bits per symbol
   Optimal compression would compress by 3.542218 percent
   Chi square: symbol count=131072, distribution=51354.63, randomly exceeds
   0.00 percent of the time
   Mean = 102.130929
   Monte Carlo value for Pi is 3.708125 (error 18.03 percent).
   Serial Correlation = -0.001802
   Longest Run Symbol = 52. Run Length = 3
   Position of Longest Run = 6143 (0x17ff). Byte position 6143 (0x17ff)
```

## 8.11.14 djenrandom

djenrandom is a program used to generate synthetic test data with known defects and known min-entropy. It supports many different parameterized generator models. djenrandom is useful for testing entropy test algorithms by provided calibrated data.

djenrandom can be cloned from GitHub:

```
$ git clone https://github.com/dj-on-github/djenrandom
Cloning into 'djenrandom'...
remote: Enumerating objects: 291, done.
remote: Total 291 (delta 0), reused 0 (delta 0), pack-reused 291
Receiving objects: 100% (291/291), 166.07 KiB | 5.54 MiB/s, done.
Resolving deltas: 100% (192/192), done.
```

It is compiled with make:

```
$ cd djenrandom
$ make
gcc -c -I/usr/local/include -m64 -Wall -maes -o rdrand.o rdrand.c
gcc -c -I/usr/local/include -m64 -Wall -maes -o markov2p.o markov2p.c
gcc -c -I/usr/local/include -m64 -Wall -maes -o djenrandom.o djenrandom.c
gcc -I/usr/local/include -m64 -Wall -maes   -c -o djenrandommodel.o
djenrandommodel.c
gcc -I/usr/local/include -m64 -Wall -maes   -c -o aes128k128d.o
aes128k128d.c
gcc -c -I/usr/local/include -m64 -Wall -maes -o cmac.o cmac.c
gcc -I/usr/local/include -m64 -Wall -maes -L/usr/local/lib  rdrand.o
markov2p.o djenrandom.o djenrandommodel.o aes128k128d.o cmac.o -o
djenrandom -lm
```

Make install puts the code in /usr/local/bin:

```
$ sudo make install
cp djenrandom /usr/local/bin
```

```
$ djenrandom -h
Usage: djrandom [-bsvhn] [-x <bits>] [-y <bits>] [-z <bits>] [-c <generate
length>]
        [-m <|pure(default)|sums|biased|correlated|normal|sinbias|markov_2_
        param|file>] [-l <left_stepsize>]
        [-r <right_stepsize>] [--stepnoise=<noise on step>] [--bias=<bias>]
        [--correlation=<correlation>] [--mean=<normal mean>]
        [--variance=<normal variance>]
        [--pcg_state_16=<16|32|64>] [--pcg_generator=<LCG|MCG>] [--pcg_
        of=<XSH_RS|XSH|RR]
        [--sinbias_offset=<0.0 to 1.0>] [--sinbias_amplitude=<0.0 to 1.0>]
        [--sinbias_period=<samples per cycle>]
        [--p10=<probability of 10 transition] [--p01=<probability of 01
        transition>]
        [--states=<integer of number of states in the markov chain>]
```

```
[--sigmoid=<flat|linear|sums|logistic|tanh|atan|gudermann|erf|
algebraic]
[--min_range=<float less than max_range>][--max_range=<float greater
than min_range>]
[-o <output_filename>] [-j <j filename>] [-i <input filename>]
[-f <hex|binary|01>]
[-J <json_filename>] [-Y <yaml_filename>]
[--bpb=<binary bits per byte>]
[-k <1K_Blocks>] [-w [1..256]]
[-D <deterministic seed string>]
```

Generate random bits with configurable non-uniformities.
  Author: David Johnston, dj@deadhat.com

-m, --model=<pure(default)|sums|biased|correlated|lcg|pcg|xorshift|norm
al|file>
            Select random source model

Step Update Metastable Source model (-m sums) Options

  -l, --left=<left_stepsize>       stepsize when moving left as a fraction of
                                   sigma_m.
  -r, --right=<right_stepsize>     stepsize when moving right as a fraction
                                   of sigma_m.
  --stepnoise=<noise on step>      variance of the noise on stepsize. e.g.
                                   0.00001.

Biased model (-m biased) Options

  --bias=<bias>                    bias as a number between 0.0 and 1.0.
                                   Only for biased or markov model

Correlated model (-m correlated) Options

  --correlation=<correlation>      Correlation with previous bit as a number
                                   between -1.0 and 1.0.
                                   Only for correlation or markov model

Sinusoidally Varying Bias model (-m sinbias) Options

```
--sinbias_amplitude=<0.0 to 1.0>      Amplitude of the variation of the
bias between 0.0 and 1.

                                      Only for sinbias model
--sinbias_offset=<0.0 to 1.0>         Midpoint Offset of the varying bias
                                      between 0.0 and 1.0.
                                      Only for sinbias model
--sinbias_period=<samples per cycle>  Number of samples for a full cycle
of the sinusoidally

                                      varying bias. Only for sinbias model
```

Two Parameter Markov model (-m markov_2_param) Options

```
--fast                  Use a fast version on the generator.
      and one set of:
--p10=<0.0 to 1.0>      The probability of a 1 following a 0,
                        default 0.5
--p01=<0.0 to 1.0>      The probability of a 0 following a 1,
                        default 0.5

      or
--bias=<0.0 to 1.0>         The ones probability, default 0.5
--correlation=<-1.0 to 1.0>  The serial correlation coefficient,
                            default 0.0

      or
--entropy=<0.0 to 1.0>    The per bit entropy, default 1.0
--bitwidth=<3 to 64>      The number of bits per symbol
```

Sigmoid Markov model (-m markov_sigmoid) Options

```
--states=<n>            The number of states in the Markov Chain
--sigmoid=<curve>       Curve name, one of: flat, linear, sums,
                         logistic, tah, atan,
                        gudermann, erf or algebraic, default linear
--min_range=<float>     The start of the range of the curve. Usually
                        between -5.0 and -2.0
--max_range=<float>     The end of the range of the curve. Usually
                        between 2.0 and 5.0
```

Normal model (-m normal) Options

```
  --mean=<normal mean>          mean of the normally distributed data.
                                Only for normal model
  --variance=<normal variance>  variance of the normally distributed data
```

Linear Congruential Generator model (-m lcg) Options

```
  --lcg_a=<LCG multipler term>  Positive integer less than lcg_m
  --lcg_c=<LCG additive term>   Positive integer less than lcg_m
  --lcg_m=<LCG modulo term>     Positive integer defining size of the group
  --lcg_truncate=<lower bits to truncate>    Positive integer
  --lcg_outbits=<Number of bits per output>    Positive integer
```

Permuted Congruential Generator model (-m pcg) Options

```
  --pcg_state_size=<state size of PCG>  16 ,32 or 64
  --pcg_generator=<Generator Algorithm> MCG or LCG
  --pcg_of=<Output Function>            XSH_RS or XSH_RR
```

XorShift model (-m xorshift) Options

```
  --xorshift_size=[state size of xorshift]  32 or 128
```

General Options

```
  -x, --xor=<bits>            XOR 'bits' of entropy together for each
                              output bit
  -y, --xmin=<bits>           Provides the start of a range of
                              XOR ratios
                              to be chosen at random per sample
  -z, --xmax=<bits>           Provides the end of a range of XOR
                              ratios to be
                              chosen at random per sample
  -s, --seed                  Nondeterministically seed the internal RNG
                              with /dev/random
  -D, --detseed <seed string> Deterministically seed the internal RNG
                              with the given string
  -n, --noaesni               Don't use AESNI instruction.
```

```
  -c, --cmax=<generate length>    number of PRNG generates before a reseed
  -v, --verbose                   output the parameters
```

File Options

```
  -o <output_filename>            output file
  -j, --jfile=<j filename>        filename to push source model internal
                                  state to
  -i, --infile=<input filename>   filename of entropy file for file model
  -f, --informat=<hex|binary|01>  Format of input file.:
                                        hex=Ascii hex(default),
                                        4 bit per hex character.
                                        binary=raw binary.
                                        01=ascii binary.
                                        Non valid characters are ignored
  -J, --json=<JSON filename>      filename to output JSON information of
                                  the data to
  -Y, --yaml=<YAML filename>      filename to output YAML information of
                                  the data to
  -k, --blocks=<1K_Blocks>        Size of output in kilobytes
```

Output Format Options

```
  -b, --binary                    output in raw binary format
  --bpb                           Number of bits per byte to output in binary
                                  output mode.
                                  Default 8 bits.
  -w, --width=[1...256]           Byte per line of output
```

The most important option of all

```
  -h, --help                      print this help and exit
```

Examples of using djenrandom are scattered throughout the book.

# 8.12  Entropy Assessment Summary

The entropy assessment requirement tends to be quite involved, requiring lab work to collect raw entropy data. A track, IID or non-IID, needs to be chosen, but it is strongly recommended to choose the non-IID track. Software tools are needed to analyze the data for prerequisite quality, to provide the statistical results needed for an entropy report, and to format data for the NIST analysis programs. Heuristic and mathematical arguments for the noise source entropy need to be made within an entropy justification report. Raw entropy data needs to be analyzed with the NIST EA tools to establish the full set of H numbers and the final assessed entropy. The full entropy report must be written, which is described in the next chapter.

# CHAPTER 9

# Entropy Source Validation Certification

Most FIPS modules will require an RNG (random number generator) for things like key and nonce generation and so will require entropy certification for the noise source within the RNG.

FIPS references SP800-90A for the random number generator requirements. SP800-90C is still in draft form at the time of writing, and SP800-90B is in a revision process and so will have some updates in the 2024–2025 time period.

SP800-90B is the standard concerned with noise sources, the online and offline testing of noise sources, and the conditioning of entropy into full entropy data for use by an SP800-90A DRBG.

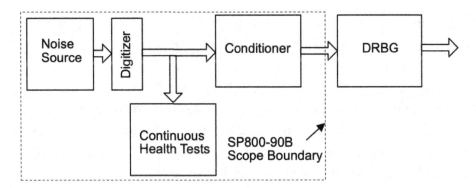

***Figure 9-1.*** *SP800-90B Scope*

The noise source is the first element in the chain of functions in an RNG complying to SP800-90A and B. The noise source is on the left of Figure 9-1. The entropy source is comprised of the noise source, digitizer, CHTs, and conditioner, all of which are specified in SP800-90B. FIPS 140-3 requires compliance to SP800-90B by getting an ESV (Entropy Source Validation) certification for any entropy source within the module. NIST Entropy

161

© David Johnston and Richard Fant 2024
D. Johnston and R. Fant, *Designing to FIPS-140*, https://doi.org/10.1007/979-8-8688-0125-9_9

Source Validation (ESV) certification is a peer certification program to the NIST CAVP algorithm certification program. An ESV certificate asserts that a particular entropy source design and implementation is compliant with SP800-90B.

Algorithms are deterministic and precisely defined, making them straightforward to validate. Entropy sources contain both deterministic and nondeterministic parts, and the design is not precisely defined within SP800-90B. So ESV certification requires a very different set of procedures and arguments compared to CAVP/ACVTS certifications.

Chapter 8 addresses entropy assessment, and this is one of the evaluations that are required for ESV certification. The additional tasks relate to showing compliance with all the other relative **shall** statements within SP800-90B and FIPS 140-3 Implementation Guidance (IG).

# 9.1  CST Labs and Prerequisites

To earn an ESV certificate, it is necessary to engage with a CST Lab (see Chapter 11). Fees for ESV certification tend to be much higher than those for CAVP certification.

One prerequisite for getting an ESV certificate is to get CAVP certificates for the approved cryptographic algorithms used within the entropy source. The CAVP certifications should be included in the agreed statement of work (SOW) with the CST Lab.

The algorithms to certify within an SP800-90B entropy source are typically the cryptographic algorithms used within the conditioner. This is typically HMAC, HASH, AES-CMAC, or AES-CBC-MAC. The conditioner may include a derivation function which must be included in the testing such as Hash_df or Block_Cipher_df.

There are a number of steps to achieve ESV certification, including noise source statistical characterization, documenting the design and heuristic entropy properties of the noise source, documenting the design and standards compliance of the CHTs, and conditioning chain and publishing a PUD (public use document).

# 9.2 ESV Certification Activities

Activities that arise during ESV certification include

1. Testing of unprocessed random raw entropy data from the noise source. See Section 8.8 of this book.

2. Testing of restart data.

3. Documenting the design.

4. Documenting the theory for how the design generates entropic data.

5. Documenting the claims and test results and showing how the design complies with SP800-90B.

6. Writing a PUD (public use document).

7. The CST Lab prepares an EAR (Entropy Assessment Report), eventually submitting the PUD and EAR to NIST on your behalf.

# 9.3 Noise Source Characterization

A noise source is a circuit that takes environmental noise and converts it to nondeterministic bits that form the start of an SP800-90 chain of processing to form an RNG. There are three primary claims that are made for the noise source – the entropy rate ($H_{submitter}$), the entropy source type physical (P) or nonphysical (NP), and the entropy statistical property of being IID (Independent and Identically Distributed) or non-IID.

The $H_{submitter}$ claim and the IID claims are tested with statistical test entropy algorithms (EA) defined in SP800-90B. A non-IID claim does not need validating, since it is the default condition for a noise source, and a claim of a source being IID is an extraordinary claim that needs justification.

# 9.4 Physical vs. Nonphysical Noise Sources

A noise source is naturally a physical thing. It senses noise from the physical environment and turns it into a stream of bits. There are several common forms of noise source, including ring oscillators, metastable collapse source (found in Intel CPUs, for instance), noise sampling sources (common in communication systems with radios), and a variety of designs that are some combination of these designs. A design of this sort is a physical source, and the submission guidelines require that it be designated a physical (P) source in the design document and PUD.

The nonphysical noise sources are implemented as software – hence the "nonphysical" part and which take advantage of nondeterministic behavior in the computer hardware. In effect, it measures the nondeterministic side effects of normal computer operations. The primary example is a Linux program called **jent** (jitter entropy) at `www.chronox.de/jent.html` that extracts entropic data from the intrinsic nondeterministic jitter of crystal oscillators on CPU motherboards. This sort of source is required to be designated a nonphysical (NP) source in the design documentation and PUD.

# 9.5 IID vs. Non-IID Sources

IID noise sources, despite being technically impossible, are an allowed class of noise source in SP800-90B. IID means Independent and Identically Distributed, meaning each symbol is drawn from the same distribution and is statistically independent from other symbols from the source. In the case of a binary source, there are only two points in the distribution (P(0) and P(1)), which means each binary symbol has some defined bias, and only some defined bias. Since the first I in IID stands for "Independent," there can be no correlation or algorithmic connection between the value of a bit and the value of any other bits.

The alternative is a non-IID source, where statistical dependence between the symbols from the source is allowed. For most noise sources, non-IID is the correct choice.

When you claim to have an IID source, SP800-90B Section 5 (Testing the IID Assumption) defines a set of algorithms to test the data from the source to establish whether or not it is IID. The tests are run over permutations of the data, as defined in SP800-90B Section 5.1 (Permutation Testing). For IID data, rearranging the data should not significantly alter the statistics. This test applies the Fisher-Yates shuffle 10,000 times and looks for significant variation in the results of the defined test statistics. There are 11 test statistic algorithms in SP800-90B Section 5.1.1 through 5.1.11 which are run using the permutation testing method defined in 5.1. In addition, Section 5.2 defines two tests in 5.2.1 and 5.2.2 for nonbinary data (data with symbols of 2 or more bits each) and in

5.2.3 and 5.2.4 two tests for binary data. Finally, there is the test in 5.2.5 that is run on data from both binary and nonbinary sources. The tests in 5.2 are not used with the permutation testing defined in 5.1.

If the IID tests pass successfully, there is then a single MCV (most common value) test defined in 6.3.1 that determines the entropy rate of the data. Section 6.1 of SP800-90B directs you to use the MCV test with an IID source.

# 9.6 Entropy Rate Claims and Non-IID Testing

For a non-IID source, there is a set of ten non-IID tests that are used, documented in Section 6.3.1 through 6.3.10 in SP800-90B. Rather than being tests with a pass/fail result, or a measurement of entropy, these tests claim to return a lower bound that is guaranteed to be below the actual min-entropy of the data.

In practice, the tests are not theoretically or practically sound. Simple testing with synthesized data of known entropy through serial correlation shows the tests both overestimate and underestimate the min-entropy, and the amount of underestimation can be very large. In a practical noise source design that generates data with a known amount of min-entropy, the min-entropy you can claim may be significantly lower following testing with the non-IID tests, and you will later have to accommodate these lower entropy rates in the conditioner design, which is discussed in Section 9.11.

# 9.7 Symbol Size Reduction

For a source that generates multi-bit symbols, it is common that not all bits in a symbol carry the same amount of entropy. For example, an ADC (Analog-to-Digital Converter) that is converting a Gaussian distributed signal to a binary number, or a time counter, measuring the time between some event, the lower-order bits of the resulting multi-bit symbols will contain more entropy.

For example, we can make a million normally distributed numbers with the djenrandom program to model the sort of data we might see when sampling a Gaussian noisy process:

```
$ djenrandom -s -m normal --mean=64 --variance=50 -k 1024
```

A snippet of the output looks like this:

```
75.76952079
63.45727370
56.10489539
58.37774171
79.53258167
68.77384133
70.15885987
56.83300958
61.17572458
71.44448399
```

We can split off the integer part with an awk script:

```
$ cat normawk.awk
BEGIN { FS = "\." }
    { print \$1 }
```

Then we can use a program dec2bin to turn each integer into a binary byte. Putting this together into a Linux shell pipeline, we get

```
$ djenrandom -s -m normal --mean=64 --variance=50 -k 1024 | awk -f normawk.
awk | dec2bin > normalbytes.bin
```

Looking at the output as hex, we can see that the bytes are far from being uniform:

```
$ bin2hex -w 16 normalbytes.bin | head
3E393E393F39443B3247443D41534542
39354C353A424642423C3E443E3A3940
3C3A3B4B4142393E38413F464038473F
433E3E3B404846433E3E333841343C4A
2C33493941493D3C463C3A3D3F41384C
4C402F3D44473F394C473E3A3C3C372D
413C434238454B3D463A473A3B4D413C
3F44434D3C3F42343A334640403C3134
3B3B4549413E443D363E4145383E3342
443E4F3F4A47473E37373E3F3A414431
```

Since the symbols are 8 bits, the min-entropy is easy to calculate using djent. The entropy rate turns out to be about 51%.

```
$ djent -b -l 8 normalbytes.bin  | grep "Min Entropy"
Min Entropy (by max occurrence of symbol 40) = 0.518534
```

However, it's clear that the bits are correlated when we look at the bytes in binary with the correlation being greater between the higher-order bits:

```
$ bin201 -w 8 normalbytes.bin | head
00111110
00111001
00111110
00111001
00111111
00111001
01000100
00111011
00110010
01000111
```

Using subfield, we can keep the lower 4 bits and throw away the upper 4 bits:

```
$ subfield -b 0 -w 4 -s 8 normalbytes.bin | bin2hex -w 8 | head
0E090E090F09040B
0207040D01030502
09050C050A020602
020C0E040E0A0900
0C0A0B0B0102090E
08010F060008070F
030E0E0B00080603
0E0E030801040C0A
0C03090901090D0C
060C0A0D0F01080C
```

This is showing the 4-bit symbols, each encoded in a full byte. Computing the min-entropy now gives a similar value:

```
$ subfield -b 0 -w 4 -s 8 normalbytes.bin | djent -b -l 8 | grep "Min
Entropy"
  Min Entropy (by max occurrence of symbol e) = 0.492131
```

Djent is measuring the entropy rate per bit over 8 bits, while the actual symbol size is 4, so the entropy rate is 0.492131x2 = 0.984262.

Trying this while truncating to bit widths from 8 down to 1 and computing the entropy, we see the following:

```
8: Min Entropy (by max occurrence of symbol 40) = 0.518534
7: Min Entropy (by max occurrence of symbol 40) = 0.518534
6: Min Entropy (by max occurrence of symbol 0) = 0.518534
5: Min Entropy (by max occurrence of symbol 0) = 0.518531
4: Min Entropy (by max occurrence of symbol e) = 0.492131
3: Min Entropy (by max occurrence of symbol 6) = 0.374409
2: Min Entropy (by max occurrence of symbol 2) = 0.249616
1: Min Entropy (by max occurrence of symbol 0) = 0.124727
```

Calculating the entropy rate for the actual symbol sizes from 8 down to 1, we get

```
8: 0.518534
7: 0.592610
6: 0.691379
5: 0.829654
4: 0.984262
3: 0.998424
2: 0.998464
1: 0.997816
```

There is no additional entropy in the upper 3 bits, and they can be safely discarded. Since 4 is a more convenient number of bits to work with in a computer than 5, and there is little entropy difference between the lower 5 bits and the lower 4 bits, it would be reasonable to reduce the symbol size to 4 bits.

Section 6.4 of SP800-90B permits an RNG with a noise source generating multi-bit symbols to eliminate some of the bits in each symbol so that only higher entropy bits are retained and the resulting entropy rate is increased. The specification asks that the bits of a symbol be ranked by how much entropy they contain, and then some numbers of the highest ranked bits are chosen and the remainder discarded.

The specification permits other ways of reducing symbol size to be used, providing an adequate justification is given in the documentation. In such a justification, showing the change in entropy for a given amount of truncation, as is done earlier, would be a way of justifying the chosen truncation amount.

Keep in mind that the SP800-90B non-IID tests can only operate on symbols that are 8 bits or less. So, there is no gain to be had by reducing the symbol size to larger symbols than 8.

# 9.8  Restart Testing

The restart test is an algorithm defined in SP800-90B Section 3.1.4 where the noise source is started 1000 times, and each time it is restarted, the first 1000 symbols from the noise source are collected. Restarting the noise source can be accomplished by either power cycling the circuit or resetting the circuit.

The 1000 samples of 1000 bits are put into a 1000 by 1000 matrix. A second matrix is made by transposing the rows to columns.

A test defined in 3.1.4.3 of SP800-90B, dubbed the "sanity check," looks for the MCV (most common value) in the rows and columns. If the noise source is putting out similar data sequences at power on or reset, this will show up as a common value repeating more often than expected for the given entropy level in the rows, columns, or both.

Once the sanity check is passed, the entropy lower bound tests in 6.1 (for the IID track) or 6.2 (for the non-IID track) are run over both the row data and column data. This gives two additional entropy lower bound estimates **H_r** and **H_c**.

Restart testing can be done on a single device at a single operating condition (temperature, voltage, etc.). It is common to do the restart testing on a device running in normal room conditions. For more details on the "restart" EA program, please see Chapter 8 of this book.

# 9.9 Skipping Initial Symbols

Correlation between the starting sequences from a noise source can be a normal part of the operation of a noise source. This could however lead to the restart sanity check failing. Provided the RNG design skips those initial symbols, it is acceptable to also skip those bits in the restart data. The text of SP800-90B says, *"Note that an entropy source, in its real-world use and during restart testing, may inhibit outputs for a time immediately after restarting in order to allow any transient weak behavior to pass."* The "entropy source" here includes the noise source, digitizer, conditioner, and CHTs, so any skipping of initial bits should be within the entropy source boundary to strictly comply. Software used to format the collected restart data should accommodate skipping initial bits if necessary. The `restart_slicer` program listed in 1.14 allows skipping a request number of initial symbols.

# 9.10 Conditioning Chain Analysis

1. *HMAC*: FIPS 198 with FIPS 180 (SHA2) or FIPS 202 (SHA3)

2. *CMAC*: SP800-38B with FIPS 197 (AES)

3. *CBC-MAC*: Described in Appendix F of SP800-90B

4. Any hash function in FIPS 180 (SHA2) or FIPS 202 (SHA3)

5. *Hash_df*: Specified in SP800-90A using any of the hash functions in FIPS 180 or FIPS 202

6. *Block_Cipher_df*: Specified in SP800-90B with FIPS 197 (AES)

These are the approved conditioning algorithms. When used correctly, these will meet the specification. In addition, vendor-defined conditioning algorithms can be used in a chain of conditioning algorithms provided that the last conditioner in the chain is a vetted conditioning component listed in 3.1.5.1.1. as shown in Figure 9-2.

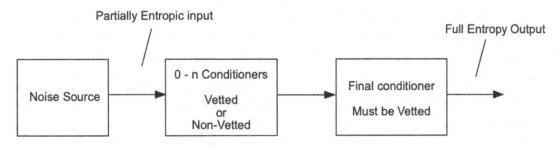

**Figure 9-2.** *Conditioner Chain*

# 9.11 Entropy Calculations for a Vetted Conditioning Component

Four parameters are used in the entropy calculations $n_{in}$, $n_{out}$, $n_w$, and $h_{in}$. Two of these parameters are a function of the algorithm you choose for the conditioner and are given in Table 1 in 3.1.5.1.1 in SP800-90B. For convenience, that table is shown in Figure 9-3.

**Table 1 The narrowest internal width and output lengths of the vetted conditioning functions.**

| Conditioning Function | Narrowest Internal Width ($nw$) | Output Length ($n_{out}$) |
|---|---|---|
| HMAC | hash-function output size | hash-function output size |
| CMAC | AES block size = 128 | AES block size = 128 |
| CBC-MAC | AES block size = 128 | AES block size = 128 |
| Hash Function | hash-function output size | hash-function output size |
| Hash_df | hash-function output size | hash-function output size |
| Block_Cipher_df | AES key size | AES key size |

**Figure 9-3.** *SP800-90B Table 1, Width and Output Length of Approved Conditioners*

The $n_{in}$ parameter is determined by your conditioner design. It is the number of bits that is input to the conditioner for each output of $n_{out}$ bits. The $h_{in}$ parameter should be chosen with attention given either to the assessed entropy rate of the noise source, when the input comes from the noise source, or to the calculated entropy of a preceding conditioner chain element if the input to the conditioner comes from another conditioner.

Typically, you will set $n_{in}$ to the number of bits necessary at the input to get full entropy at the output. We can think of this in terms of *extraction ratio* where the extraction ratio is the ratio of the number of bits of data into the conditioner to the number of bits of data out of the conditioner. The ratio should always be greater than one, so that more data is going in than is coming out.

Common and practical extraction ratios are between 3:1 and 6:1 although there is no rule forbidding operation outside that range if the assessed entropy rate permits it.

SP800-90B Section 3.1.5.1.2 gives the equations for assessing the output entropy rate of a vetted conditioner as a function of the four parameters.

$$h_{out} = \text{Output\_Entropy}(n_{in}, n_{out}, nw, h_{in})$$

where $\text{Output\_Entropy}(n_{in}, n_{out}, nw, h_{in})$ is described as follows[4]:

1.  Let $P_{high} = 2^{-h_{in}}$ and $P_{low} = \frac{(1 - P_{high})}{2^{n_{in}} - 1}$.
2.  $n = \min(n_{out}, nw)$.
3.  $\psi = 2^{n_{in} - n} P_{low} + P_{high}$
4.  $U = 2^{n_{in} - n} + \sqrt{2\, n (2^{n_{in} - n})\ln(2)}$
5.  $\omega = U \times P_{low}$
6.  Return $- \log_2(\max(\psi, \omega))$

*Figure 9-4.*  *From SP800-90B Section 3.1.5.1.2: Output Entropy Equations*

This will return the number of bits of min-entropy in the $n_{out}$ bits from the conditioner. To get the entropy rate (the entropy per bit), divide $h_{out}$ by $n_{out}$. This does not tell you directly how big to make $n_{in}$ or how big to make the extraction ratio.

For the different conditioner options, we can use these equations to evaluate what entropy rate is needed at each extraction ratio from 2x to 6x. Tables 9-1 to 9-4 are the result of increasing $n_{in}$ by 128 for each entry, and the entropy rate of the input was increased until the entropy output rate met the full entropy criteria.

***Table 9-1.*** *With CBC-MAC and CMAC, $n_{out} = 128$*

| Extraction Ratio | $n_{in}$ | $n_{out}$ | Required Min-Entropy Rate |
|---|---|---|---|
| 2 | 256 | 128 | 0.5998 |
| 3 | 384 | 128 | 0.3999 |
| 4 | 512 | 128 | 0.2999 |
| 5 | 640 | 128 | 0.2399 |
| 6 | 768 | 128 | 0.2000 |

***Table 9-2.*** *With HMAC-SHA256, $n_{out} = 256$*

| Extraction Ratio | $n_{in}$ | $n_{out}$ | Required Min-Entropy Rate |
|---|---|---|---|
| 1.5 | 384 | 256 | 0.7306 |
| 2.0 | 512 | 256 | 0.5480 |
| 2.5 | 640 | 256 | 0.4384 |
| 3.0 | 768 | 256 | 0.3653 |
| 3.5 | 896 | 256 | 0.3131 |
| 4.0 | 1024 | 256 | 0.2740 |
| 4.5 | 1152 | 256 | 0.2436 |
| 5.0 | 1280 | 256 | 0.2192 |
| 5.5 | 1408 | 256 | 0.1993 |
| 6.0 | 1536 | 256 | 0.1827 |

**Table 9-3.** *With HMAC-SHA384, $n_{out} = 384$*

| Extraction Ratio | $n_{in}$ | $n_{out}$ | Required Min-Entropy Rate |
|---|---|---|---|
| 1 1/3 | 512 | 384 | 0.7968 |
| 1 2/3 | 640 | 384 | 0.6375 |
| 2 | 768 | 384 | 0.5312 |
| 2 1/3 | 896 | 384 | 0.4553 |
| 2 2/3 | 1024 | 384 | 0.3984 |
| 3 | 1152 | 384 | 0.3542 |
| 3 1/3 | 1280 | 384 | 0.3188 |
| 3 2/3 | 1408 | 384 | 0.2898 |
| 4 | 1536 | 384 | 0.2656 |
| 4 1/3 | 1664 | 384 | 0.2452 |
| 4 2/3 | 1792 | 384 | 0.2277 |
| 5 | 1920 | 384 | 0.2125 |
| 5 1/3 | 2048 | 384 | 0.1992 |
| 5 2/4 | 2175 | 384 | 0.1875 |
| 6 | 2304 | 384 | 0.1771 |

**Table 9-4.** *With HMAC-SHA512, $n_{out} = 512$*

| Extraction Ratio | $n_{in}$ | $n_{out}$ | Required Min-Entropy Rate |
|---|---|---|---|
| 1.25 | 640 | 512 | 0.8386 |
| 1.5 | 768 | 512 | 0.6974 |
| 1.75 | 896 | 512 | 0.5977 |
| 2 | 1024 | 512 | 0.5230 |
| 2.25 | 1152 | 512 | 0.4649 |
| 2.5 | 1280 | 512 | 0.4184 |

(*continued*)

***Table 9-4.*** (*continued*)

| Extraction Ratio | $n_{in}$ | $n_{out}$ | Required Min-Entropy Rate |
|---|---|---|---|
| 2.75 | 1408 | 512 | 0.3804 |
| 3 | 1536 | 512 | 0.3487 |
| 3.25 | 1664 | 512 | 0.3219 |
| 3.5 | 1792 | 512 | 0.2989 |
| 3.75 | 1920 | 512 | 0.2790 |
| 4 | 2048 | 512 | 0.2615 |
| 4.25 | 2175 | 512 | 0.2462 |
| 4.5 | 2304 | 512 | 0.2325 |
| 4.75 | 2432 | 512 | 0.2203 |
| 5 | 2560 | 512 | 0.2092 |
| 5.25 | 2688 | 512 | 0.1993 |
| 5.5 | 2816 | 512 | 0.1902 |
| 5.75 | 2944 | 512 | 0.1820 |
| 6 | 3072 | 512 | 0.1744 |

# 9.12  Entropy Calculations for a Non-vetted Conditioning Component

Section 3.1.5.1.2 of SP800-90B gives the following equation for non-vetted conditioners.

h' is the assessed entropy from the previous stage, either the noise source or a preceding conditioner. The output_entropy() function is the same function used for vetted conditioners in 3.1.5.1.1.

$$h_{out} = min\left(Output\_Entropy\left(n_{in}, n_{out}, nw, h_{in}\right), 0.999 n_{out}, h' \times n_{out}\right)$$

As can be seen, it is impossible to get full entropy out of a non-vetted conditioner using the SP800-90B criteria since the maximum entropy of hout is 0.999nout when h is perfect.

Possible reasons to use a non-vetted conditioning component include the following:

1. Including a post-quantum conditioning component that is not part of SP800-90

2. Including more recent conditioners based on more current research topics like nonmalleable conditioners

The state of research on conditioning components has moved on a long way since the algorithms in SP800-90B were considered optimal. One strategy in taking advantage of this research involves using them as non-vetted conditioning components that are followed with a vetted conditioning component. A design can only claim full entropy if it's using a vetted conditioner. However, a design could claim 0.9 bits of entropy per bit of output using a non-vetted conditioner.

# 9.13  Choosing a Conditioner

The choice of conditioner is not arbitrary. The different vetted conditioning algorithms are not created equally, and the security properties of some are not ideal.

The first three conditioners are keyed MACs, meaning the algorithm has two inputs, the data input into which the entropic input data goes and a key input. The key input should be a number that can be expected to be independent of the noise source input. A good choice is to pass some simple constants through a hash or AES to make a fixed key for the key input to the MAC. It would be a mistake to make a key that would be characteristic of the output of the noise source.

The fourth choice of conditioner is any NIST-approved hash function. These do not require a key and so create no challenge to justify that your choice of key is independent of the source.

These four conditioners are all good options. They come with good theoretical understanding that they are good conditioners with suitable security properties for a random number generator.

The last two options are the derivation functions (df) that are specified in SP800-90A. These were written with SP800-90A and so predate SP800-90B by several years. The constructions are complex and unnecessary. They were written during the same period of time that the backdoored Dual-EC-DRBG was added to SP800-90A, and the odd design choices seen in the derivation functions can be looked at in that light.

The hash_df is mandatory for use with the hash DRBG in SP800-90A. This is one of a few good reasons not to choose the hash DRBG.

The Block_Cipher_df is not mandatory with the block cipher DRBG. The simpler constructs defined for vetted conditioners in SP800-90B can be used with the block cipher and HMAC DRBGs.

Considerations for algorithm choices can be driven by the available acceleration hardware. A system with an AES block cipher in hardware might choose CMAC or CBC-MAC for the conditioner and the CTR-DRBG for the DRBG. A system with hash or HMAC acceleration might choose to use the vetted HMAC conditioner from SP800-90B with the HMAC DRBG from SP800-90A.

Data availability sizes can be a factor. A 128-bit CTR-DRBG requires 256 bits to perform a reseed operation. A 256-bit CTR-DRBG requires 384 bits to perform a reseed operation. The environment may or may not provide exactly that amount of full entropy data. The hash and HMAC DRBGs and conditioners are tolerant of variable size inputs, and this may or may not matter for the application.

# 9.14  SP800-90B Compliance Report

When submitting documentation for ESV certification to the CST Lab, the primary document is the SP800-90B Compliance Report. By contrast, when the CST Lab submits the ESV request to NIST, the Entropy Assessment Report (EAR) and the PUD are the primary documents. These names can be misleading and are not interchangeable.

The Compliance Document is written by the entropy source designer and may or may not be proprietary; it is not normally shared with NIST. The EAR is written by the CST Lab (see Chapter 11) and is a proprietary document shared exclusively with NIST. The Compliance Report is normally a superset of the EAR since it can cover much more than entropy assessment such as how the design of the entropy source meets the SP800-90B requirements along with the additional requirements described in IG (Implementation Guidance) Sections D.J and D.K NIST entropy evaluators have stated they much prefer reading the shorter EAR instead of the longer Compliance Report.

The Compliance Report contains a number of things:

1. Identification of the device or devices being certified

2. Statement of the noise source type – physical (P) or nonphysical (NP)

3.  Statement of $H_{submitter}$

4.  Operating conditions of the device(s)

5.  A description of the noise source

6.  A description of the APT and RCT implementation

7.  A description of any vendor-defined CHTs, including details of how they comply with SP800-90B

8.  A description of the failure modes of the source and explanation of how the CHTs detect those failure modes

9.  A description of the conditioning chain

10. Analysis of the output entropy of the conditioning chain as a function of the input entropy rate

11. A heuristic analysis of the entropy rate from the noise source

12. Where appropriate, simulation results of the noise/entropy source

13. A description of the entropy data collection procedure and apparatus

14. Results of ea_restart testing

15. Results of ea_iid or ea_non_iid testing

16. A summary of the claims and results

17. A shall-mapping table, linking every **shall** statement in SP800-90B, IG DJ and IG DK, to text in the document that shows how the **shall** statement has been satisfied

A CST Lab should be able to assist in making an SP800-90B compliance document meet NIST's expectations. The work to create an SP800-90B Compliance Report is substantial and can exceed the effort involved in creating supporting documentation for a full FIPS module certificate. The Compliance Report for the Intel entropy source runs to over 80 pages and is accompanied with a peer-reviewed journal paper by one of the authors of the report, supporting the claims made in the report.

# 9.15  Public Use Document

The public use document is a simpler document that, as the name suggests, is public. It describes to a user of the certified entropy source a few things:

1.  The identity of the certified entropy source

2.  The operating conditions required for the source, such as voltage and temperature or, in the case of a nonphysical source, the operating system and hardware platform

3.  How to get random numbers from the source

4.  How to run the self-tests

5.  How failure is signaled by the source

6.  Links to the CAVP and ESV certifications

At the time of writing, NIST has a template and guidance available at `https://csrc.nist.gov/Projects/cryptographic-module-validation-program/entropy-validations/documents` for SP800-90B compliance reports and public use documents.

# 9.16  Parameter Summary Table

Near the start of an entropy compliance report, it is good to include a summary table of the test parameters, entropy claims, and other details contained within the report. This is appreciated by CST Labs since they do not have to dig through the report to find these numbers.

An example summary table is shown in Table 9-5.

***Table 9-5.*** *Parameter Summary Table Example*

| Parameter | Name | Detail |
|---|---|---|
| Physical(P) | Noise Source Type | The noise source is a physical circuit implemented in a silicon chip |
| Non-IID | IID Claim | The noise source does not product IID data since there is serial correlation arising from the feedback network in the noise source |
| 0.85 | $H_{original}$ | Result of ea_non_iid entropy assessment |
| 0.6 | $H_{submitter}$ | Entropy level above which the noise source will always generate, set with additional margin to set RCT and APT H value with sufficient margin to yield a reliable test |
| 0.84 | Hr | Row assessment of ea_restart |
| 0.87 | Hc | Column assessment of ea_restart |
| 0.6 | Assessed Entropy | $min(H_{submitter}, H_{original}, H_r, H_c)$ |
| 0.6 | RCT H | |
| 0.001 | RCT Alpha | |
| 67 | RCT C | |
| 0.6 | APT H | APT H set to match assessed entropy |
| 0.01 | APT Alpha | |
| 60 | APT C | |
| 1 | Conditioning Chain Length | There is a single vetted conditioning component |
| AES-CMAC | Conditioner Algorithm | |
| 4 | Extraction Ratio | The ratio of input data to output data from the conditioner |
| 0.2999 | Min Conditioner Input Entropy Rate | The minimum entropy rate to the conditioner necessary to achieve full entropy at the output with epsilon $< 2^{-32}$ |

# 9.17 Continuous Health Tests

SP800-90B Section 4 describes the health tests, and 4.4.1 and 4.4.2 describe two mandatory continuous health tests, the RCT (Repetition Count Test) and APT (Adaptive Proportion Test).

The RCT is defined in Section 4.4.1 of SP800-90B. The second paragraph refers to H as "the assessed min-entropy of a noise source." H is then used in the subsequent equations that calculate the parameters of the test.

---

### 4.4.1   Repetition Count Test

The goal of the Repetition Count Test is to quickly detect catastrophic failures that cause the noise source to become "stuck" on a single output value for a long period of time. It can be considered as an update of the "stuck test" that was previously required for random number generators within FIPS-approved cryptographic modules. Note that this test is intended to detect a total failure of the noise source.

Given the assessed min-entropy $H$ of a noise source, the probability[9] of that source generating $n$ identical samples consecutively is at most $2^{-H(n-1)}$. The test declares an error if a sample is repeated $C$ or more times. The cutoff value $C$ is determined by the acceptable false-positive probability $\alpha$ and the entropy estimate $H$ using the following formula

---

**Figure 9-5.** *From SP800-90B Section 4.4.1: the definition of the RCT*

Unfortunately, the assessed min-entropy of the noise source is not the min-entropy of the noise source. It is a lower bound below the actual min-entropy. This means that the error rate calculations in the standard are not valid since they are not based on the actual min-entropy of the source.

In addition, the assessed min-entropy is calculated from either the vendor claimed $H_{submitter}$ or the output of the EA programs run over data from a single device. The former can and should be padded to accommodate variation across devices. The latter tests are statistically unreliable.

In practice, if the text of SP800-90B is taken at face value, the calculations for the RCT will be wrong with the min-entropy from the source either being higher or lower than the H assumed in the RCT calculations.

In CHT design, setting the cutoff value as a function of the expected entropy of the source is problematic. The job of the CHT is to detect when the min-entropy of the noise source is too low to meet the minimum input entropy level to the conditioner necessary to achieve full entropy at the output. The cutoff value of the test should be a function of that minimum, with some margin added to accommodate the natural imperfect cutoff of the test, rather than as a function of how well the noise source performed on the day of testing.

You can envisage a noise source that is excellent, usually achieving an assessed min-entropy rate above 0.99 with a conservative conditioner only needing an entropy rate of 0.3. The specification would expect you to set H for the CHT to 0.99, which would fail frequently when the noise source entropy varies due to environmental conditions, while always being sufficient to exceed the minimum required input entropy to the conditioner.

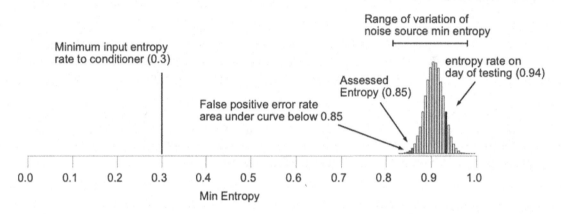

**Figure 9-6.**  *RCT Problem*

As shown in Figure 9-6, the quality of data from the testing is drawn from the distribution of quality across all the devices. It may turn out to be better or worse on the day of testing with the device that is chosen. A close-to-uniform noise source will get $H_{original}$ close to 0.85. If the distribution of noise quality across devices has any significant area below 0.85, the false positive error rate of the CHT will be very high, shown by the shaded area below 0.85 on the diagram.

There are two simple approaches to work around this problem. The first is just to make H in the RCT (and maybe in the APT) not equal to the assessed entropy.

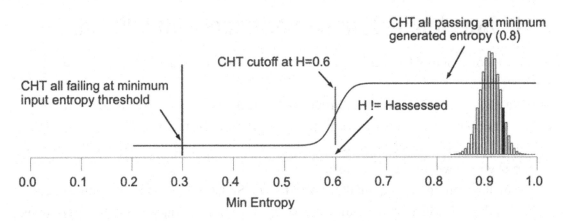

***Figure 9-7.*** *RCT Solution*

In Figure 9-7, H has been set to 0.6 so that at the point where the entropy is too low to achieve full entropy at the output of the conditioner, the CHT is failing all data samples from the noise source. When the noise source is operating normally and the entropy quality is in the expected range, the CHT is passing all samples from the noise source. The false positive and false negative error rates are negligible.

The second approach is essentially the same. Do not be honest about $H_{submitter}$. Instead, set $H_{submitter}$ to the place where you want the CHT cutoff to be. In Figure 9-7, if $H_{submitter}$ was set to 0.6, then it would be the lowest of the H numbers, and so the assessed entropy would be 0.6 and H in the RCT tests would be able to be both equal to the assessed entropy and also 0.6.

This discussion has arisen with CST Labs where the report chose a sensible value for H in the RCT test and the CST Lab expected H equal to the assessed min-entropy. The conclusion was to add text to the report to clearly justify the selection of H used for the RCT. When the second method (setting $H_{submitter}$ low) was tried, we got questions about why it was so low.

Again, it helps to be very clear in the document why $H_{submitter}$ is low. For example, a statement similar to the following quote, if used in the entropy compliance report, could help avoid unnecessary confusion (and delays) with the NIST reviewers:

> *4.4.1 requires the RCT H to be equal to the assessed entropy and H*
> *set to Horiginal would yield a very high false positive error rate.*
> *By setting $H_{submitter}$ lower than the range of entropy expected*
> *from the source and above the minimum input entropy rate to the*
> *conditioner low false positive and false negative error rates*
> *can be achieved with the CHTs*

# 9.18 Developer-Defined Continuous Health Tests

Section 4.5 of SP800-90B describes "developer-defined alternatives to the continuous health tests."

The RCT and APT tests may be implemented directly or as a subset of a developer-defined test. If you can show that your developer-defined test rejects all samples that the RCT and APT would reject, then you can claim you have implemented the RCT and APT as part of your developer-defined test.

If you have implemented the RCT and APT, the SP800-90B Section 4.5 requirements do not apply to the developer-defined health tests. This is not clear in SP800-90B but has been verbally confirmed by NIST staff, and they have indicated that it will be clarified in a future revision of the standard.

The reason to implement a developer-defined health test is because the RCT and APT are not adequate tests for your noise source. In practice, the RCT and APT are rarely good tests for any noise source, and so developer-defined continuous health tests are close to mandatory.

The RCT tests capture long strings of the same symbol. There is a cutoff value, and when the length of the currently repeating symbol exceeds that cutoff, an error is raised. This would capture stuck-at events within a noise source, where it outputs the same value continuously. It could also arise from a source with strong positive serial correlation, for example, from sampling a ring oscillator too fast.

In the case where the noise source is outputting strongly negative serial correlation, the output will keep changing. For example, a binary noise source outputting data with a serial correlation coefficient of –1.0 would be outputting 010101010101010101... continuously.

Both the RCT and APT tests would be blind to this failure mode. The RCT is seeing run lengths never exceed its cutoff. The APT is seeing the chosen symbol appears 50% of the time, which to the APT is perfect.

A technically correct fix for the APT is to make the symbol size of the APT tests larger, say, 8 bits. Then data from a negatively correlated source would output 0xAA or 0x55 much more frequently, and this would be detected by the APT. Similarly, a positively correlated source would output 0x00 or 0xFF more frequently, and this would be detected by the APT. However, while it is not stated in the specification, CST Labs have assumed that the symbol size of the APT and RCT will be equal to the symbol size of the noise source.

So as with the H values for the tests, the specification and interpretation of the standard force poor engineering choices on the RNG designer.

For this reason, the simplest approach is to directly implement the RCT and APT, which will sit there not detecting real errors, but you can use it to claim compliance, while the real test work is done with the developer-defined test that you must also implement.

Section 4.5 of SP800-90B lists two specific requirements.

The first is a strange requirement, since it is essentially asking that the developer-defined health test perform the same task that the mandatory RCT performs.

---

a.   If a single value appears more than $\lceil 100/H \rceil$ consecutive times in a row in the sequence of noise source samples, the test **shall** detect this with a probability of at least 99 %.

---

The RCT sets the cutoff at $C = 1 + \dfrac{-log_2\alpha}{H}$ , while the developer-defined health test requirement sets it at $C > \dfrac{100}{H}$ .

The developer requirement asks for a false positive of 1% (since the positive detection rate is 99%), so that equates to alpha of 0.01 in the RCT calculation.

Comparing the two values for H from 0.1 to 0.9 with alpha = 0.01, we see the overlap in Table 9-6.

*Table 9-6.  Overlap of SP800-90B Section 4.5a with RCT*

| H | RCT C | Developer-Defined Test C |
|---|-------|--------------------------|
| 0.1 | 68 | 1000 |
| 0.2 | 35 | 500 |
| 0.3 | 24 | 334 |
| 0.4 | 18 | 250 |
| 0.5 | 15 | 200 |
| 0.6 | 13 | 167 |
| 0.7 | 11 | 143 |
| 0.8 | 10 | 125 |
| 0.9 | 9 | 112 |

The cutoff for the developer-defined test requirement is always greater than the RCT cutoff for that same alpha. Therefore, if the RCT is directly implemented or the developer-
defined test is a superset of the RCT, this requirement is already met. Strings of repeating symbols exceeding the developer-defined cutoff requirement will already have been detected by the RCT.

You may be designing a great test for known failure modes of the source while knowing the RCT is taking care of the stuck-at cases, but this requirement has you also bending the test to testing for cases that will already have been detected. This is a bad requirement that should not be in the specification.

There has been active discussion about this within the CMUF. NIST has indicated verbally that if you have implemented the RCT and APT, the Section 4.5 requirements do not apply to the developer-defined health tests. This is not clear in SP800-90B but has been verbally confirmed by NIST staff, and they have indicated that it will be clarified in a future revision of the standard.

The second requirement on developer-defined health tests is the following:

> b.  Let $P = 2^{-H}$. If the noise source's behavior changes so that the probability of observing a specific sample value increases to at least $P* = 2^{-H/2}$, then the test **shall** detect this change with a probability of at least 50 % when examining 50 000 consecutive samples from this degraded source.

Just as the first requirement is an analog of the RCT, this requirement is an analog of the APT, requiring that a single symbol being more frequent than it should be for some entropy level be detected by the test.

This requirement makes the same mistake that is made with the RCT and APT definition, defining the change to be detected in terms of the assessed entropy, rather than in terms of the lower bound of min-entropy that is the failure point of the conditioner.

Designing CHTs is outside the scope of this book, but approaches taken by the authors for developer-defined health tests include pattern counting a range of bit patterns at multiple bit lengths and bounding the acceptable frequency and computing statistics like bias, run length, and serial correlation during runtime and looking for combinations of those statistics that equate to there being sufficient entropy from the source.

# 9.19  Example ESV Certificates

At the time of writing, there are well over 100 ESV certificates issued. They can be searched on the NIST website here:

https://csrc.nist.gov/projects/cryptographic-module-validation-program/entropy-validations/search?ipp=25

An example ESV certificate can be seen at

https://csrc.nist.gov/projects/cryptographic-module-validation-program/entropy-validations/certificate/57

**Entropy Certificate #E57**

| Details | |
| --- | --- |
| Implementation Name | Intel DRNG Entropy Source |
| Standard | SP 800-90B |
| Description | Intel DRNG Entropy Source |
| Version | DRNG4.2_PIC6_V1, RNG_ES_GEN3.0 |
| Noise Source Classification | Physical |
| Reuse Status | Open for Reuse |

| | Operating Environments | Vetted Conditioning Component CAVP Certificates |
| --- | --- | --- |
| Entropy Per Sample: 0.6 bits Sample Size: 1 bit | • Intel Intel® Agilex™ F-Series and I-Series SoC FPGAs Intel® Agilex™ AGF 019 / AGF 023 / AGI 019 / AGI 023 SoC FPGAs | • A3212 (AES-CBC-MAC) |

***Figure 9-8.***  *From the NIST website: ESV Certificate E57 Vendor Information*

# 9.20  Multiple Operating Environments

An ESV certificate may contain more than one operating environment (OE). In the case of software, this may refer to different computer hardware and operating systems that the software may run on. In the case of a physical noise source design, this could refer to the same design within multiple different chips.

An existing ESV certificate can be amended with additional operating environments provided the RNG design is the same. Amending an ESV certificate with additional operating environments typically costs significantly less than getting a new ESV certificate. Amending ESVs this way has been recommended by NIST, since it takes less time and effort for the NIST staff compared to processing a new ESV submission.

ESV certificate #14 shows 16 different operating environments within a single ESV certificate:

```
https://csrc.nist.gov/projects/cryptographic-module-validation-program/
entropy-validations/certificate/14
```

# CHAPTER 10

# FIPS and Documentation

As the reader may have observed by now, there are numerous official publications related to FIPS; these span a range from high-level overview specifications to low-level cryptographic algorithm standards. All of these documents must be considered when designing a FIPS validated module. This chapter will highlight some of the more important and thus commonly referenced FIPS publications.

## 10.1 FIPS 140-3 PUB

FIPS 140-2 was initially published in 2001 by the National Institute of Standards and Technology (NIST) to organize the requirements and standards for cryptographic modules. The international standard ISO/IEC 19790, released in 2006, was then subsequently based on the FIPS 140-2 standard. And ironically, in 2019, FIPS 140-3 was published and in a role reversal was extensively derived from the current ISO/IEC 19790:2012 publication. While the FIPS 140 standards are free of charge, the ISO/IEC 19790 does require a fee for copies.

It is important to note that the CMVP tests all cryptographic modules for adherence to the FIPS 140 standards, **not** the ISO/IEC 19790 standards. Ironically, the **FIPS 140-3 PUB** is the shortest FIPS document with only 11 pages. This shouldn't be too surprising since FIPS 140-3 is mostly based on the ISO/IEC 19790 standards. Most of the FIPS 140-3 publication is used to provide alternative requirements from those listed by the ISO/IEC 19790 and ISO/IEC 24759. These alternative requirements are in the form of Special Publications (SP) issued by the CMVP.

The ISO/IEC 19790 standards are typically only updated once every seven years. But obviously, the field of cybersecurity changes much more often as new vulnerabilities are discovered, and new technologies such as quantum computing are developed. To help facilitate the rapidly changing security landscape, the FIPS 140 standards have a companion document to clarify and expand the FIPS 140 publications; it is updated

© David Johnston and Richard Fant 2024
D. Johnston and R. Fant, *Designing to FIPS-140*, https://doi.org/10.1007/979-8-8688-0125-9_10

much more frequently by the CMVP as needed. This companion document is titled the *Implementation Guidance for FIPS 140-3 and the Cryptographic Module Validation Program.* It is commonly referred to as the "IG."

## 10.2  Implementation Guidance (IG)

To help clarify its FIPS 140 standards, NIST has published a series of documents referred to as Implementation Guidance (IG). These IGs primarily provide guidance (hence its name) on how the FIPS 140 should be interpreted. In addition, the FIPS 140 IGs will frequently expand the FIPS 140 standards by adding rules or recommendations that were not included in the ISO/IEC 19790 standard.

For example, the ISO/IEC 19790:2012 Section 7.1 specifies that if a cryptographic module has been designed to mitigate against attacks, then the module's supporting document "**shall** enumerate the attack(s) the module is designed to mitigate." However, in FIPS 140-3, this requirement is relaxed somewhat since in IG 12.A, it states Section 7.1 is only applicable if the module has publicly documented this mitigation. For example, if your cryptographic module has implemented some mitigation for an RSA attack, the designer is only required to include details of that mitigation in the module's Security Policy, if the designer has public marketing or advertising material where they claim this RSA attack mitigation. It's a very subtle but important distinction.

## 10.3  Management Manual (MM)

The main purpose of the Management Manual (MM) is to define for both CST Labs and vendors the infrastructure and management upon which the FIPS validation processes are based. Many view the MM as a "catch-all" for topics that don't fit neatly within other existing FIPS publications. Some of these MM topics include the process of how a CST Lab becomes accredited by the National Volunteer Laboratory Accreditation Program (NVLAP); this accreditation allows the CST Lab to submit FIPS certification requests to the CMVP. The MM also states the monetary fees which must be paid to NIST for each service type available. The newest section of the MM describes the Entropy Source Validation Program (ESV) uses to certify entropic designs used for random number generations.

Some of the most esoteric (and controversial) topics of the MM include the NIST definition of simulation vs. emulation; this is an important topic for many vendors since simulation may be used for cryptographic algorithm validation, while emulation cannot be.

# 10.4  CAVP Documents

These are official publications which detail how approved cryptographic should be implemented as well as validated. Many of these documents have a prefix of "SP" which stands for "Special Publication," while other (usually older) documents just have a prefix of "FIPS"; for example, "FIPS 197" is the specification for the AES algorithm, and "SP 800-38A" defines its different modes. There is at least one such document for every approved cryptographic algorithm and its modes of operation.

But please note that the list of approved cryptographic algorithms is not static. This is a constantly evolving list as older (i.e., less safe) algorithms are deprecated and newer algorithms are introduced (e.g., post-quantum safe algorithms). So please note that the data in these tables will grow stale over time.

The following tables summarize the most common algorithms by mapping each approved algorithm to its primary FIPS standard. Please note that a single algorithm may be described in multiple documents. Some of the formerly approved but now deprecated algorithms are listed as well for convenience since some of these may still be allowed to support legacy systems.

## 10.4.1  Block Ciphers and Modes

| Algorithm/Mode | Notes | Primary FIPS Standards |
|---|---|---|
| AES | Advanced Encryption Standard | FIPS 197 |
| TDEA | Triple Data Encryption Algorithm | SP 800-67 |
| ECB, CBC, CFB, OFB, CTR | AES, TDEA Modes | SP 800-38A |
| CMAC | AES, TDEA Mode | SP 800-38B |
| CCM | AES Mode | SP 800-38C |
| GCM, GMAC | AES Mode | SP 800-38D |
| XTS | AES Mode | SP 800-38E<br>FIPS 140-3 IG CI |
| KW, KWP, TKW | AES, TDEA Key Wrap | SP 800-38F |
| Skipjack | Deprecated. Decryption Only | FIPS 185 |

## 10.4.2  Digital Signatures

| Algorithm/Mode | Notes | Primary FIPS Standards |
|---|---|---|
| DSA | Deprecated. SigVer only | FIPS 186-4 |
| ECDSA, RSA | Not post-quantum safe | FIPS 186-5, FIPS 140-3 IG CF |
| ML KEM (CRYSTALS-Kyber) | Module Lattice–based key encapsulation mechanism (key exchange). Post-quantum safe | FIPS 203 |
| ML DSA (CRYSTALS-Dilithium) | Module Lattice–based DSA. Post-quantum safe | FIPS 204 |
| SLA-DSA (SPHINCS+) | Stateless hash-based DSA. Post-quantum safe | FIPS 205 |
| LMS, XMSS | Stateful hash-based digital signature scheme. Post-quantum safe | FIPS 208 |

## 10.4.3  Key Derivation Functions

| Algorithm/Mode | Notes | Primary FIPS Standards |
|---|---|---|
| KBKDF | Key-Based Key Derivation Function | SP 800-108 |
| PBKDF | Password-Based KDF | SP 800-132 |

## 10.4.4  Key Management

| Algorithm/Mode | Notes | Primary FIPS Standards |
|---|---|---|
| KAS | Key agreement scheme | SP 800-56A, FIPS 140-3 IG DA |

## 10.4.5  Message Authentication

| Algorithm/Mode | Notes | Primary FIPS Standards |
|---|---|---|
| HMAC | Keyed-Hash MAC | FIPS 198-1, SP 800-107 |

## 10.4.6  Random Number Generation

| Algorithm/Mode | Notes | Primary FIPS Standards |
|---|---|---|
| DRBG | HASH_DRBG, HMAC_DRBG, CTR_DRBG | SP 800-90A |

## 10.4.7  Secure Hashing

| Algorithm/Mode | Notes | Primary FIPS Standards |
|---|---|---|
| SHA-1 | Will be disallowed after 2025 for new FIPS modules | FIPS 180-4 |
| SHA-2 | | FIPS 180-4 |
| SHA-3 | | FIPS 202 |

# 10.5  Security Policy

The Security Policy (SP) is a nonproprietary public document that describes a FIPS validated module. The SP must contain a list of all the cryptographic services (including algorithms) contained within the module. Note that not all cryptographic services are algorithms. Consider, for example, a zeroization function which is a cryptographic service but does not have a specific algorithm associated with it. Similarly, a function which returns the cryptographic module software version number is a cryptographic service but not an algorithm. By contrast, a cryptographic algorithm might be a SHA-2 algorithm or even a non-approved cryptographic algorithm such as RC4.

The SP must also cover how the module is initialized the very first time as well as define the different user roles such as crypto officer or user. The SP must describe the Life Cycle

Assurance infrastructure used in the module's design such as internal documentation, version control, and even how the validated module is securely delivered to the end user.

## 10.6  Entropy Source Validation Public Use Document (ESV PUD)

The ESV PUD is a newly required FIPS document used to publicly describe the entropy source (ES) contained within the FIPS validated module. The PUD will include descriptions of the operational environment (OE) in which the ES operates as well as the claimed entropy rate. This is one of the shorter documents and is generally written by the vendor with the coordination of a CST Lab.

## 10.7  Entropy Assessment Report (EAR)

The EAR is a proprietary document written by an accredited CST Lab and submitted to the CMVP for an ESV certification. The EAR must describe the noise source used by the entropy source and provide a mathematical prediction of what the entropy rate should be based on the design. The EAR will also describe the continuous health tests and any data conditioning used in the entropy source. In addition, the EAR will contain the actual entropy numbers calculated by the 90B entropy assessment (EA) tools based on raw entropy data captured from the noise source. The purpose of the EAR is to defend the vendor's claim of the entropy rate generated by the entropy source. In other words, the CMVP does not define or require a minimum entropy rate for any FIPS validated module. But instead, it only requires that the vendor is able to prove and justify whatever entropy rate the vendor claims for their entropy source.

## 10.8  Post-Quantum Computing (PQC) Standards

These PQC publications are in their infancy. There is no doubt these PQC standards will morph over time as currently approved cryptographic algorithms are deprecated, and newly design PQC-safe cryptographic algorithms are tested publicly. At time of writing of this book, only one PQC standard has been approved by NIST: "SP800 208 Recommendations for Stateful Hash-based Signature Schemes". But there are 3 other standards in draft form which are expected to be approved in 2024. The best place to go for updates and more information in general on PQC and FIPS is www.nist.gov/pqcrypto.

# CHAPTER 11

# Engaging with a CST Lab

## 11.1  What Is a Cryptographic Security Testing Lab (CST Lab)?

In the United States, many taxpayers commonly use a tax consultant when annual income taxes are due to the government's Internal Revenue Service (IRS). Typically, the taxpayer will deliver their receipts, charitable donation records, pay stubs, etc., to this third-party tax consultant, also known as a certified public accountant (CPA), who then reviews the documents and applicable tax laws. In consultation with the taxpayer, the CPA then determines the best strategy to minimize the amount of income tax owed by the taxpayer and submits their report to the IRS. If the IRS requires additional information or questions the tax strategy employed, the CPA will directly negotiate with the IRS on behalf of their client until an agreement is reached.

Certifying a cryptographic module works in a similar fashion. A CST Lab can be thought of as a CPA for cybersecurity. But instead of dealing with the IRS, the lab deals with a different government agency: the CMVP. Bear in mind that while using a CPA is optional for a taxpayer, the use of a Third-Party CST Lab is required by the FIPS 140-3 standards for module validation. The list of currently accredited Third-Party CST Labs is located under the program listed as "**ITST: Cryptographic and Security Test**" at

`www-s.nist.gov/niws/index.cfm?event=directory.results`

© David Johnston and Richard Fant 2024
D. Johnston and R. Fant, *Designing to FIPS-140*, https://doi.org/10.1007/979-8-8688-0125-9_11

To carry this analogy further, the IRS allows taxpayers to use commercial software such as TurboTax to submit their tax returns without involving a CPA. The CMVP is starting to do likewise for some of the steps of its validation process. For example, the ACVTS can now be used by first-party labs (i.e., noncommercial CST Labs owned by the vendor) to request their own CAVP certificates. This means the vendor can request their own test vectors from the ACVTS server and generate their own response files for submission to the CAVP without using a Third-Party CST Lab. This can save the vendor time and money. Similarly, an Automated Entropy Source Validation Test System (ESVTS) is currently under development to further remove responsibility from the Third-Party CST Labs.

The goal in automating validation and testing is to reduce the amount of time needed by the CMVP to issue a certificate for a cryptographic module without compromising its security testing. At the time of this writing, the CMVP currently has a nine-month wait time for their "Review Pending" queue. This means a module has to wait that long before it is even assigned to a CMVP reviewer. Clearly, the challenge here is that with serious attacks by malicious users increasing all the time, waiting nine months for an official certificate does not facilitate a timely response to these security threats.

# 11.2  What CST Lab Services Are Typically Offered?

Different CST Labs will usually offer different services at different costs. But in general, most CST Labs offer service in the following broad categories:

- FIPS 140-3 consultation and training

- Writing of Request for Guidance (RFG) documentations to the CMVP

- Requesting of CAVP certificates

- Requesting of ESV certificates

- Generation of the reports required for first-time CMVP cryptographic module certification

- Generation of the reports required for ESV certification

- Resubmitting an updated, but previously validated, module for revalidation by the CMVP

## 11.2.1 FIPS 140-3 Consultation and Training

While FIPS 140-3 training is a fairly easy-to-understand category, FIPS 140-3 consultation is not. The FIPS Implementation Guidance document specifies that a CST Lab may not perform any validation testing on a cryptographic module where the CST Lab has designed or written any part of the module. Basically, if you design a product, you shouldn't be the one to validate it because of potential conflicts of interest. While this is a sound *Quality Assurance* mindset, it can be difficult for a vendor and CST Lab to find the exact line between consulting and designing. One strategy used by CST Labs to avoid crossing that line is for the Lab to provide a FIPS 140-3 Gap Analysis service. This service typically examines a vendor's proposed module design and identifies any areas that are not compliant with FIPS. As part of the service, the CST Lab can provide clarification of FIPS standards and guidelines.

However, this is frequently a less-than-satisfactory solution; for example, imagine a CPA asking their client to propose a tax strategy for their retirement when the client is ignorant of the finer points of the tax laws.

One way to address this issue is for the vendor to take FIPS training. A vendor designing a FIPS-compliant module cannot do so in complete ignorance of the FIPS standards. It will cost the vendor far more in time, consultation fees, and product redesigns than simply having the FIPS training prior to designing the module. In addition, the more FIPS training a vendor has, the better they can work with their CST Lab to find an acceptable solution for their cryptographic module. Another (and much more expensive) option is to use two different CST Labs: one for the design consultation and a different one for the module validation testing.

## 11.2.2  Generation of CAVP and ESV Certificates

Another service offered by CST Labs is generating documentation and submitting requests for ESV, CAVP, or CMVP certificates. As a reminder, CAVP and ESV certification is a prerequisite for CMVP certification. That is, the CMVP certification is for the entire cryptographic module consisting of

- Entropy source analysis (i.e., ESV certificate)

- FIPS-approved and certified cryptographic algorithms (i.e., CAVP certificates)

- Numerous documents such as the Security Policy which detail and define how the operation of the module is compliant with FIPS 140-3

As stated earlier, the CMVP is now allowing First-Party CST Labs (i.e., labs internal to the vendor) to request their own CAVP certification without going to an external CST Lab. The CMVP plans to eventually allow these same First-Party CST Labs to also submit requests for ESV certification. However, CMVP certification still requires a vendor to engage with a CST Lab for the actual submission to the CMVP.

## 11.2.3  Request for Guidance

In general, a vendor is not allowed to contact the CMVP directly for any questions related to a particular module implementation. Instead, once a vendor has contracted with a CST Lab, only that CST Lab is allowed direct communication with the CMVP for questions related to that module. This formal process is known as a *Request for Guidance* (RFG). When the CMVP responds to an RFG, their response has the force of law which can be used by the CST Lab when they submit the module to the CMVP for validation. For example, if the CMVP chooses to grant an exception for a particular module from adhering to one part of the FIPS 140-3 standard, the CST Lab can reference that RFG number as part of their justification in their module submission.

On the other hand, if a vendor has a general question not related to any particular module implementation, the vendor can submit an Informal RFG to the CMVP. For example, the vendor can informally ask questions of the CMVP related to a clarification of some standard through the CMUF venue described in Section 11.6. Any response from the CMVP is considered nonbinding by the CMVP, and their answer may change in the future.

# 11.2.4  Submission Type for Cryptographic Module Certification

The CMVP allows a CST Lab to use different submission types for modules undergoing validation. These different submission categories have corresponding levels of difficulty as well. For example, most of the modules submitted to the CMVP for validation are new to FIPS. But some are revalidation of existing module which are about to reach their sunset date.

The most common categories of CMVP submissions are described next, while Table 11-1 contains the full summary for submission types:

- Those modules new to FIPS are known as a **Full Submission** (a.k.a. "FS"). This means the module must be completely validated for all aspects of the module type (hardware, software, hybrid, or firmware) and security level (1–4). These typically take the longest time to validate since everything is subjected to evaluation.

- By contrast, those modules that are already certified are known as **Update Submissions**. These submission types (a.k.a. "UPDT") are where less than 30% of the security aspects of the module have changed from the previous version. These types of submissions are placed in the same review queue as an FS but typically take less time because only the changed portions of the module are examined and validated.

***Table 11-1.*** *CMVP Submission Types*

| Submission Type | Abbreviation | Purpose |
|---|---|---|
| Full Submission | FS | The module must be completely validated for all aspects of the module type (hardware, software, hybrid, or firmware) and security level (1–4). This is done for new modules |
| Vendor Update | VUP | These are typically updates to documentation such as vendor contact information or typos discovered in the Security Policy |
| Vendor Affirmed Operating Environment | VAOE | This is used to update the Security Policy to reflect new vendor affirmed operating environments |

*(continued)*

*Table 11-1.* (*continued*)

| Submission Type | Abbreviation | Purpose |
|---|---|---|
| Non-security Relevant | NSRL | This is used when modifications have been made to the hardware, software, or firmware of an existing module which do not impact any security related items |
| Algorithm Update | ALG | After a module is validated, any FIPS-approved algorithms which were not supported by the CAVP when the module was submitted may now be officially tested using the ACVTS. Note that code changes within the module are not permitted if using the ALG submission type |
| Operating Environment Update | OEUP | This is used when a new OE is added to an existing validated module. CAVP testing will need to be done on the module in this new OE |
| Rebrand | RBND | This is used when the original owner of a validated module gives written permission to another vendor to change the name/description of the validated module provided the module itself has not change. The exact terms of the rebrand must be explicitly stated in the approval letter. For example: Is a rebrand of the rebrand allowed? Can more OEs be added to the rebrand? Etc. |
| Port Sub Chip | PTSC | This is used when a previously validated sub-chip cryptographic system is reused to another single-chip implementation. There can be no security-related modification to the sub-chip allowed in this submission scenario |
| Update | UPDT | Request to extend the life of a validated module by updating its sunset date. This basically extends the life of the certificate by 5 years assuming there are no changes done to the cryptographic module |
| | | These submission types (a.k.a. "UPDT") are where less than 30% of the security aspects of the module have changed from the previous version |

(*continued*)

***Table 11-1.*** (*continued*)

| Submission Type | Abbreviation | Purpose |
|---|---|---|
| Common Vulnerabilities and Exposures | CVE | This is used by the CMVP to fast-track any security changes made to an existing cryptographic module which has had cybersecurity vulnerabilities identified in the field. This type of submission will hopefully shorten the waiting time in the Review Pending queue |
| Algorithm Transition | TRNS | This is used when a vendor wants to transition an algorithm to an updated or new algorithm. This is useful when a FIPS-approved algorithm is deprecated and moves to a non-approved state |
| Physical Enclosure | PHYS | This is used when the physical enclosure of the cryptographic module has been updated. This submission scenario is only allowed if no operational changes have been made to the module |

The full details of these submission types are described in the FIPS 140-3 Management Manual located at

`https://csrc.nist.gov/CSRC/media/Projects/cryptographic-module-validation-program/documents/fips%20140-3/Draft%20FIPS-140-3-CMVP%20Management%20Manual%2009-18-2020.pdf`

# 11.3 FIPS Module Life Cycle Timeline

Earning a FIPS 140-3 certificate for a cryptographic module is not a trivial task. While different CST Labs have different timelines depending on the complexity of the cryptographic module and the FIPS experience of the lab, there are some phases common to all labs. Table 11-2 shows some of the steps involved for an FS submission. The durations shown are based on years of empirical experience and gleaning data from the CMVP MIP website. The durations are estimates for a Security Level 2 hardware module.

As a guide to measuring complexity of a cryptographic module, keep in mind that software is usually easier to validate than hardware. For example, a Security Level 1 software module is typically less complex (and so takes less validation time) than a Security Level 4 hardware module. In addition, if a modification is needed to correct a software module's noncompliance, that update is usually far easier to do than fixing a similar issue on a hardware module.

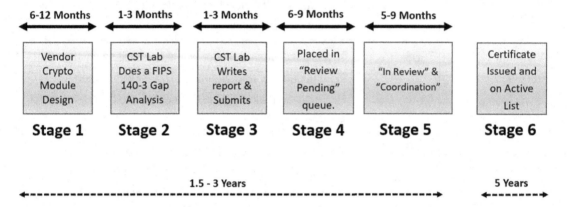

**Table 11-2.** *FIPS Validation Timeline*

| Stage | Comment[1] |
|---|---|
| 1 | This is a wild guess since it depends on complexity, vendor experience, and engagement with the CST Lab |
| 2 | This could be much less if the CST Lab was involved in stage 1 |
| 3 | This is typically done by the CST Lab |
| 4 | This changes frequently depending on resourcing at the CMVP (and the occasional government shutdown) |
| 5 | This depends on the experience of the CMVP reviewer and how well the reports were written by the CST Lab |
| 6 | The module can be revalidated on or near the sunset date |

---

[1] Your Mileage May Vary

# 11.3.1  "In Review" and "Coordination"

Assuming a CST Lab has done their due diligence in stages 1–4, then the most important (and time-consuming) part of the validation process is the "In Review" and "Coordination" stages. When a module enters the "In Review" stage, CMVP reviewers are assigned to evaluate the module and its documentation. There is typically one NIST CMVP reviewer and one CCCS CMVP reviewer assigned.[2] Because the CMVP has many experts in mathematics, cryptography, digital logic design, and physics, module reports which are clear, well written, and technically accurate will generally pass through this stage faster than poorly written reports.

After a module exits the "In Review" stage, the CMVP reviewers will contact the CST Lab: this is the start of the "Coordination" stage. During "Coordination," the CMVP reviewers will email specific questions to the CST Lab regarding the content of the reports. The email response from the CST Lab is considered to be the first round of Coordination. Ideally, only a single round of Coordination is needed if the module is not complex, or the reports are well written. However, even if the module and reports are perfect, the CMVP has a standard list of "cookie cutter" questions they will ask. These questions are fairly generic and could apply to all module types and security levels. For example, *"How long does it take to completely zeroize the module?"* Or *"Was the entropy assessment based only on the vendor-provided documentation or did the CST Lab perform any original research?"* If these generic questions are the only types of comments the CMVP reviewers have, then the CST Lab did an excellent job. Typically, a single "Coordination" round will take anywhere from two to six weeks depending on the resource loading at the CMVP.

On the other hand, if there are multiple "Coordination" rounds, the module could be stuck in "Coordination" for much longer. There are examples of module being in "Coordination" for almost a year. In other words, a poorly documented module could spend more time in "Coordination" than in the initial "Review Pending" queue.

If multiple rounds are required, then there may be a fundamental misunderstanding on the part of the CST Lab of what the CMVP reviewers are actually asking, or the technical knowledge of the CST Lab may be lacking. In those cases, it is not unusual for the CST Lab engineers to request a conference call with the CMVP reviewers and the

---

[2] NIST: National Institute of Standards and Technologies. CCCS: Canadian Centre for Cyber Security

vendor's design team to expedite the question/answer rounds. If a CST Lab takes more than 90 calendar days in responding to a comment from the CMVP, the module will be placed "On Hold".

## 11.4  When Should a CST Lab Get Involved?

In general, a module designer should engage with a CST Lab as early as possible in the product's development life cycle. Not doing so can cost a vendor millions of dollars and delay product release. Early engagement with a CST Lab for a software cryptographic module is less critical than with a hardware cryptographic module since modifying software takes far less effort and time than changing a hardware design.

A word of warning: Adding FIPS compliance as a "feature" to a cryptographic product as an afterthought is a poor design strategy. There are many examples in the industry where cryptographic hardware designers have postponed involvement of a CST Lab until the very last step of their development phase. The CST Lab then found some subtle violation of the FIPS standard that prevented the hardware module from being CMVP certified, and because of the significant redesign cost, the product was canceled.

## 11.5  Strategy for Picking a CST Lab

There are several things besides cost to consider when deciding on which CST Lab to use. Most of this information is publicly available on the CMVP website which has an easy-to-use search function for its website located at `https://csrc.nist.gov/projects/cryptographic-module-validation-program`.

Data points to look for should include

- How long has this CST Lab been in business? When does their current CST Lab accreditation expire and are they planning on renewing it?

- How many certificates for my specific module type (hardware, software, hybrid, security level, etc.) has this lab done in the last 24–36 months? The FIPS requirements can change quarterly via its IG updates, so it's important to have a CST Lab which is current with the latest rules.

- Typically, how long are their modules in "In Review" and "Coordination"? This is important information. See section 11.3.1.

- What other vendors has the lab worked with in the past? This is public information.

- Is this lab involved with any working groups or forums such as Cryptographic Workshops, CMUF (Cryptographic Module User Forum), and ICMC (International Cryptographic Module Conference)? These types of groups are focused primarily on understanding FIPS 140-3 compliance and CMVP policy changes for cryptographic modules. If a CST Lab is not engaged with these types of forums, it should raise a concern about their ability to certify a module.

- Has this lab ever had a certificate revoked? If so, why? The vast majority of module certificates spend their lives on the active list for five years before reaching their sunset date and transitioning gracefully to the historic list. However, some certificates are put on the revoked list before their sunset date. The most common reason for this is because a FIPS cryptographic algorithm is no longer considered secure by the CMVP and so is obsoleted, which means any module based on that algorithm is also unsecure and revoked. However, another reason a certificate can be revoked is if a serious security vulnerability is found in the module after it is released into the field.

In general, having a good relationship with a Third-Party CST Lab is as important as having a good relationship with an automobile mechanic familiar with your vehicle. You might not need them every day, but when something breaks (or a question comes up), you want someone knowledgeable quickly involved before wasting additional money.

# 11.6  CMVP, ICMC, and CMUF

The CMVP ensures that cryptographic modules which claim FIPS compliance do in fact adhere to the various standards which defined FIPS 140-3. As mentioned earlier, the CMVP is an agency which was created in 1995 by the US and Canadian governments for cryptographic module validation. The US representative of the CMVP works under the jurisdiction of the US Department of Commerce. This is an important fact since it differentiates the CMVP from the US National Security Agency (NSA). The main purpose of the NSA is intelligence gathering with an emphasis on network and data security, while the Department of Commerce is focused on commerce (hence its name). This means the CMVP is open to making changes to the FIPS standards based on vendor feedback. One forum where this can happen is the International Cryptographic Module Conference.

The International Cryptographic Module Conference (ICMC) is a security conference with global impact. The ICMC was started in 2013 by Atsec Information Security for the purpose of training, sharing insights, and discussing strategies involving cryptographic module validation. The ICMC meets annually and is targeted toward those involved with the development of certified modules based on standards like the FIPS 140 series. The conference is generally well attended by many different CST Labs, vendors who develop cryptographic modules, and various government agencies such as NIST. Various parallel technical tracks allow the participants to choose which topics to attend. Popular topics usually include entropy analysis and FIPS updates.

Following the success of the first annual ICMC and the strong demand of continuing the discussions initiated there on a more frequent basis, the Cryptographic Module User Forum (CMUF) was created to serve as an important resource for developers or testers of FIPS-compliant modules. Atsec hosts the CMUF portal free of charge to its members and serves as a liaison to the International Organization for Standardization (ISO). The CMUF members include representatives of the US and Canadian government standards organizations as well as CST Labs. Most importantly, it also includes vendors who develop OEM hardware and software cryptographic modules. This means the vendors have direct contact with the CMVP using the CMUF. This allows the vendors to share feedback about FIPS processes or standards that are unduly hindering the vendor's ability to sell to their customers. Based on this feedback, the CMVP can (and has) modify their FIPS validation process to remove or reduce unnecessary obstacles. In addition, the CMUF members can provide feedback on draft copies of upcoming standards or modifications to ISO/IEC 19790 and 24759, upon which FIPS 140-3 is based.

# Index

## A

Actual min *vs.* lower bound min
    entropy, 119
Adaptive Proportion Test (APT), 123
    continuous health tests, 181–183
    developer-defined continuous health
        tests, 184–186
Analog-to-Digital Converter (ADC), 165
Approved/non-approved algorithms
    block ciphers, 44–49
    CAVP website, 44
    cryptographic requirements, 43
    DRBG algorithms, 68
    message authentication code, 57–60
    NIST hash function, 50–58
    web page/document/CAVP
        links, 60–67
Automated Cryptographic Validation
        Protocol (ACVP), 20
    certificate headings, 107
    communication protocol, 77
    JSON schema, 107
    Skylake-28 DTNG algorithm, 107, 108
Automated Cryptographic Validation Test
        System (ACVTS), 20, 87
    components, 77
    CST (*see* Cryptographic Security
        Testing Lab (CST Lab))
    Demo Server/Production Server, 79
    demo vectors
        AES-ECB test request JSON, 90–97
        expected response files, 97–102

expected/response JSON file,
    106, 107
request files, 103–105
request/response files, 89
high-level steps, 77
process flow, 77
production environment, 85
test vectors, 79, 80
verdict types, 78

## B

Block ciphers
    AES encrypts and decrypts, 45
    authenticated encryption modes
        (AEAD modes), 48
    authentication modes, 48
    ciphertext stealing privacy modes, 48
    confidentiality modes, 47, 48
    DF (derivation function), 72
    privacy modes, 47
    publications, 191
    Skipjack, 44
    SP800-131Ar2 document, 44, 45
    TDEA/DES links, 47, 48
    Two-Key TDEA, 46
    types, 44

## C

Certified public accountant (CPA), 195
Cipher-Based Message Authentication
        Code (CMAC), 48, 58, 59

© David Johnston and Richard Fant 2024
D. Johnston and R. Fant, *Designing to FIPS-140*, https://doi.org/10.1007/979-8-8688-0125-9

Cipher Block Chaining Message
    Authentication Code (CBC-MAC),
    48, 57, 58
Continuous Health Test (CHT), 123, 181
Critical Security Parameter (CSP), 20, 25
Cryptographic algorithm self-test
    (CAST), 15, 26
Cryptographic Algorithm Validation
    Program (CAVP), 20, 87
    ACVTS (*see* Automated Cryptographic
      Validation Test System (ACVTS))
    CST Lab, 198
    definition, 75
    First-Party Lab *vs.* Third-Party Lab
      cipher option, 83
      CVP tester accreditation, 84
      First Party CAVP Lab, 81–84
      Lab type, 82
      setting up First-Party Lab, 84–86
      17ACVT laboratory, 85
      test vectors, 83
      time savings, 83
    implementation under test (IUT), 75
    known-answer test (KAT), 75
    official publications, 191–193
    persistent problem, 80
    validation process flow, 81
      tools, 81
    Windows-based tool, 76
Cryptographic boundary, 4–9, 13, 23
Cryptographic modules, 1, 40, 189, 205, 206
Cryptographic Module User Forum
    (CMUF), 206
Cryptographic Module Validation
    Program (CMVP)
    CST Lab, 196, 198, 199, 203–205
    security accreditation programs, 2
    validated module website, 12

Cryptographic Security Testing
    Lab (CST Lab)
    ACVTS process flow, 77
    broad categories, 196
    cipher option templates, 83
    CMVP/ESV certification, 198
    CMVP/ICMC/CMUF, 205
    commercial software, 196
    consultation, 197
    data points, 204
    implementation details, 89
    module designer, 204
    module life cycle timeline
      In Review/Coordination stages, 203
      validation, 202
    Request for Guidance (RFG), 198
    submission types, 199–201
    taxpayer, 195
    test vectors and submit responses, 87
    Thris-Party CST Lab, 76
    time savings, 83
    training, 197
    update submissions, 199
    vendor information, 88, 89

**D**

Data Encryption Standard (DES), 47
Deterministic Random Bit
    Generators (DRBGs), 51, 68, 72
Differential Power Analysis (DPA), 25, 68
Documentation, FIPS, 189

**E**

Entropy assessment (EA), 133, 160
    actual min *vs.* lower bound min
      entropy, 119

bias and serial correlation, 116
certification/cryptographic context, 110
collision entropy, 110
definition, 109
ESV certificate (*see* Entropy Source Validation (ESV) certification)
file formats, 126, 127
finite binary sequences, 111, 112
$H_{submitter}$, 121–123
IID (*see* Independent and Identically Distributed (IID))
max entropy/Hartley entropy, 109
MCV analysis, 117, 118
min entropy, 110
min entropy variation, 114, 116
noise source data, 124–126
non-full/non-IID binary sequences, 112–117
probability mass function histogram, 111
programs (*see* Software tools)
Rényi entropy, 109, 110
Shannon entropy, 109
skipping initial data, 127
Entropy Assessment Report (EAR), 177, 194
Entropy Source Validation (ESV), 20, 198
    calculations $n_{in}$, $n_{out}$, $n_w$, and $h_{in}$, 171–175
    certification activities, 163
    conditioners, 176, 177
    conditioning chain algorithms, 170
    continuous health tests, 181–183
    CST Lab, 162
    derivation functions (df), 176
    developer-defined continuous health tests, 184–186

E57 vendor information, 187
Gaussian noisy process, 165
IID *vs.* Non-IID sources, 164
jent (jitter entropy), 164
noise source characterization, 163
non-IID tests, 165
non-vetted conditioners, 175
operating environment (OE), 187
parameter summary table, 179, 180
physical *vs.* nonphysical noise sources, 164
public use document, 179
restart testing, 169
skipping initial symbols, 170
SP800-90B compliance report, 177, 178
SP800-90B scope, 161
symbol size reduction, 165–169
vetted conditioning component, 171
websites, 187
Entropy Source Validation Public Use Document (ESV PUD), 194
Entropy Source Validation Test System (ESVTS), 196
Environmental Failure Protection (EFP), 20
Environmental Failure Testing (EFT), 20
Error Detection Code (EDC), 20
Extendable output functions (XOF), 49, 53

**F**

Federal Information Processing Standards (FIPS 138-3)
    boundaries, 4
    categories, 3
    CMVP (*see* Cryptographic Module Validation Program (CMVP))
    CMVP reviewers/user forums, 3

Federal Information Processing
Standards (FIPS 138-3) (*cont.*)
compliance, 4
cryptographic algorithms, 19, 20
definition, 1
documentation, 20, 189
executive-level consumption, 18, 19
finite state model requirement, 28
firmware module, 8, 9
firmware *vs.* software, 13
FSM (*see* Finite state model (FSM))
generic block diagram, 5
hardware module, 5, 6
hybrid firmware module, 11, 12
hybrid hardware module, 9
hybrid software module, 9, 10
logical interfaces, 4
module definitions, 3
modules, 23
    hypothetical hardware module, 24
    logical and physical ports, 24, 25
module website, 12
noninvasive, 15
OCS ROM code, 5
security requirements, 14–16
software module, 6, 7
standards, 2
zeroization service, 18
Finite state model (FSM)
approved service state, 39
approved state/service states, 31
approved/unapproved system state, 29
CAVP request vectors/recover, 40
equivalent, 31
FIPS mandatory states, 29
mandatory states (*see*
    Mandatory states)
non-approved services, 40

raw data collection state, 41
simplified system, 30
transition table, 31, 34
user state/approved state, 31
FIPS 140-3, *See* Federal Information
Processing Standards (FIPS 140-3)

**G**

Galois Counter Mode (GCM), 49
Galois Message Authentication Code
(GMAC), 48, 57

**H**

Hardware security modules (HSMs), 23
Hash-Based Key Derivation
Function (HKDF), 67
Hash functions (NIST)
cSHAKE128 and cSHAKE256, 54
definition, 49
ParallelHash, 55
permission table, 50
SHA-1, 51
SHA3 algorithms, 52
SHA224/SHA256, 51
SHA384, SHA512, SHA512/224, and
SHA512/256, 52
SHAKE128 and SHAKE256, 53
SHAKE algorithms, 54
SP800-90A DRBGs
disallowed hashes, 57
Implementation Guidance (IG), 56
permitted options, 56
SP800-131A Rev 2, 50
TupleHash, 54
Hash Message Authentication
Code (HMAC), 60, 72

H ($H_{submitter}$) numbers/assessed entropy
  assessed entropy, 123
  $H_{bitstring}$, 122
  heuristic analysis and testing, 121
  $H_{initial}$, 122
  $H_{original}$, 122
  $H_r/H_c$, 122
  test thresholds, 123

## I, J

Independent and Identically Distributed
    (IID), 163
  meaning, 119
  non-IID data, 119
  permutation testing, 120
  SP800-90B track, 120
  statistical tests, 120
Internal Revenue Service (IRS), 195
International Cryptographic Module
    Conference (ICMC), 206
ISO/IEC 19790\:2012
  finite state model, 31
  Life Cycle Assurance, 28
  self-tests, 26, 27
  zeroization, 27

## K, L

Keccak Message Authentication
    Code (KMAC), 54, 60
Key-Based Key Derivation Functions
    (KBKDFs), 60–67
Key Derivation Functions (KDFs), 71
  counter mode, 61
  double pipeline iteration mode, 63, 64
  feedback mode, 62
  FIPS 196-1 HKDF, 67
  PBKDF links, 63–67

PRF algorithms, 61
publications, 192
SP800-108 definition, 60

## M

Management Manual (MM), 190, 201
Mandatory states
  approved state, 35, 36
  bypass state, 38
  crypto officer, 34
  CSP entry state, 35
  error state, 36, 37
  general initialization state, 33, 34
  optional states, 38
  power on/off state, 33
  self-tests, 36
  user role, 35
Message Authentication Code (MAC)
  CBC-MAC, 57, 58
  classes, 57
  CMAC links, 58, 59
  HMAC links, 60
Most common value (MCV) analysis, 115,
    117, 118, 165, 169

## N

National Institute of Standards and
    Technology (NIST), 1
  FIPS 138-2, 189
  hash functions, 49
Noise source data
  entropy source model, 124–126
  file formats, 126, 127
  programs (see Software tools)
  skipping initial data, 127
Non-vetted conditioners, 140, 175

# O

Offload and Crypto Subsystem (OCS), 5
Operational environment (OE), 5, 20, 187

# P, Q

Password-Based Key Derivation
        (PBKDF), 63–67
Poor cryptographic design
    AES, 73
    Block Cipher DF (derivation
        function), 72
    CTR-DRBG algorithm, 72
    double pipeline iteration, 71
    Dual-EC-DRBG, 71
    elliptic curves, 71
    general principles, 69
    HMAC and HASH DRBGs, 72
    modern attack techniques, 70
    old/insecure algorithms, 70
    S-Box, 73
    security system, 70
Post-Quantum Computing (PQC), 194
Preoperational self-tests (POST), 17, 21, 26
Probability Mass Function (PMF), 110, 111
Pseudorandom functions (PRF), 61
Publications, FIPS, 189
    CAVP algorithms, 191
        block ciphers/modes, 191
        digital signatures, 192
        Key agreement scheme, 192
        Key Derivation Function, 192
        message authentication, 193
        random number generation, 193
        secure hashing, 193
    EAR, 194

    ESV PUD, 194
    FIPS 138-3 PUB, 189
    Implementation Guidance (IG), 190
    Management Manual (MM), 190
    PQC standards, 194
    Security Policy (SP), 193
Public Security Parameters (PSP), 21
Public use document (PUD), 162, 179

# R

Random bit generator (RBG),
        15, 19, 21, 68
Random number generator (RNG),
        34, 161, 169, 170
Repetition Count Test (RCT), 123
    continuous health tests, 181–183
    developer-defined continuous health
        tests, 184–186

# S

Security Policy (SP), 4, 6–8, 10, 26, 190, 193
Self-tests, 26, 36, 37
Sensitive Security Parameter (SSP),
        13, 15, 21, 25
Serial correlation coefficient (SCC),
        114, 115, 184
Software tools
    bin2hex, 129
    bin2nistoddball, 130
    djenrandom, 154–159
    djent, 149–154
    ea_conditioning computes, 136–141
    ea_iid computes, 141–143
    ea_non_iid computes, 143–146

ea_restart, 146–148

ea_transpose, 148

format/test random data, 128

hex2bin, 129

hexbinhex, 128, 129

NIST ea_non_iid, ea_iid, restart, 133–135

nistoddball2bin, 130

restart_slicer, 131–133

## T, U, V, W, X, Y

True Random Number Generator (TRNG), 21

Two-Key Triple Data Encryption Algorithm (TDEA), 46

## Z

Zeroization service, 18, 21, 27

Printed in the United States
by Baker & Taylor Publisher Services